Evolution
of the Bible

to Carol, a great coworker and friend. Thanks for your interest in the book.

Craig [signature]

An Integral, Evolutionary Worldview

Craig R. Vander Maas

Integral Growth Publishing
Grand Rapids, MI

Integral Growth Publishing
Grand Rapids, MI
www.integralgrowthpublishing.com

For information regarding bulk purchases of 10 or more
copies, please email: info@integralgrowthpublishing.com

For more information about the author please visit:
www.craigvandermaas.com

First Edition
ISBN 978-0-9972388-0-8 pbk

Acknowledgments

Many thanks to Rev. Joshua Holwerda, Rev. Todd Petty, Steven Lems, Dr. Richard Rotman, and, especially, Mark Lodenstein and Dr. Robert and Marcia Cross for feedback and editing advice.

Do not be conformed to this world, but be transformed by the renewing of your minds, so that you may discern what is the will of God—what is good and acceptable and perfect.

Saint Paul (Romans 12:2)

Contents

Evolution of the Bible

An Integral, Evolutionary Worldview

Preface

Although in school I learned things about history, biology, astronomy, archeology, physics, chemistry, psychology, and other disciplines, I don't think I received a lot of help in integrating all of this knowledge. Often various knowledge bases were compartmentalized, i.e., there was biological knowledge and then there was biblical knowledge, for example. If discrepancies were acknowledged, the Bible would win out. After all, how can one argue with God?!

I feel I'm a seeker of truth. I'm not one just to believe what I'm told without questioning. I want empirical evidence. I want data. Perhaps this is because of my personality (my Myers-Briggs code is INTJ), perhaps because of life experiences in which I learned that many things I was taught to believe were absolutely false, or perhaps it is partly because of my training as a clinical psychologist. My beliefs and worldview have changed significantly over the years. But despite this, my belief in God remains strong, and I remain a Christian, a follower of Jesus Christ. Spirituality is of immense importance to me, and I continue to be active in church. Some people maintain that we shouldn't question our beliefs; I emphatically disagree. I don't believe we should be a Republican or a Democrat simply because that was the way we were raised. I don't believe we should be a Christian, Muslim, Hindu, or Buddhist just because that was the way we were raised. I once attended the funeral for an elderly woman who was praised for having "never questioned her faith." I don't believe that is a virtue. I think that *true* belief requires questioning, thinking, and research. To blindly believe something out of ignorance is not virtuous. To refuse to question out of fear is cowardice. To be brainwashed is not faith. I believe we should be wary of any institution that tells us to avoid reading information that is contrary to a particular belief system, whether that institution is a Taliban madrassa or a fundamentalist Christian church. I feel that if we are open-minded and hear all sides of an issue, the truth will win out, and we don't have to fear the truth.

I have done a lot of research on various disciplines including theology, philosophy, history, anthropology, archeology, geology, physics, biology, astronomy and, of course, psychology. This series of books contains information that I feel has been important for the development of my "worldview," or actually my "universe view," which has changed tremendously over the course of my life as a result of study and research. My goal in writing this series of books is to share this information in a concise and easily understandable format. Every author needs to make decisions about what information to share in a book and what information to exclude in order to be succinct. The information that I've chosen to share for each of the topics in this book series is the information that I felt was most important for the change and development of my own worldview.

Due to the advent of the Internet, this is an interesting time in the history of mankind. Never before has so much information been so readily available. At one time, every book or manuscript was handwritten. The printing press made written materials available to a large number of individuals. Now with the Internet almost the sum total of human knowledge is available to virtually everybody. I can't imagine doing the research for this book without the Internet.

This research was important for me in getting a clear sense of the "big picture" and for developing a sense for the "meaning of life." I'm writing this series of books in order to share what I've learned. I teach for two universities; teaching and sharing of knowledge is important to me. It is particularly important for such a vital topic as this. Our worldviews contribute to how we live our lives. Collective worldviews contribute to cultures. I believe it is God's will for us to grow and to evolve as individuals and cultures. As a psychologist my job is to help people grow emotionally and spiritually. If it is a surprise to you that psychologists would be concerned with spiritual growth, note that the word "psychology" means the study of the psyche. Psyche means "soul" or "spirit."

This particular book is a summary of what I've learned about the development of the Bible, and this in turn has had a great effect on my worldview, which I would describe as "integral" (meaning I've tried to integrate information learned from many disciplines to work at finding ultimate truth) and "evolutionary" (meaning that "evolution" seems to be the word that best describes God's "logos" or divine animating principle that pervades the universe). This present book is part of a proposed series of books that will present summaries of research that contribute to my integral, evolutionary worldview.

My Early Worldview

I grew up in Grand Rapids, Michigan, a mid-sized city known in part at that time (the 1950s and 60s) for its many churches. The residents of the city at that time were largely from Dutch and Polish ancestries. The Polish were mainly Catholic, and the Dutch primarily went to various Dutch Reformed Churches. The church I grew up in was in the denomination of The Reformed Church of America. I attended a Christian parochial school which was primarily affiliated with The Christian Reformed Church, a slightly more conservative denomination that split from the Reformed Church in America in 1857.

I was blessed with a loving, middle-class family. The world outlook that I had growing up was, I think, quite typical for those with an evangelical background. One difference my Calvinist background made from many other evangelicals, however, was the belief in the doctrine of predestination. This doctrine teaches that all are inherently sinful and deserving of hell. Because of God's grace, he rescues some from the destruction that all deserve. These people are known as "the elect." They are rewarded after death with eternity in a heavenly paradise. The rest spend eternity tormented in hell. Of course we all believed that we were part of the elect. So with the worldview in which I grew up, there was a great dichotomy between people: the elect who were chosen by God to spend eternity in paradise, and those not elected who were doomed to torture in hell. What about little babies that died? The explanation I most often heard was that children who did not have the chance to give their life to Jesus would go to heaven. This also was the proposition put forth in the best-selling "Left Behind" series of books by Tim LaHaye and Jerry Jenkins. These assertions often made me wonder whether it might be best to die as a child or be aborted and thus be guaranteed eternity in heaven.

I grew up believing that the most important goal of life was to get to heaven after death. The lifetime we spend on earth is a mere blink of the eye compared to the eternity of the afterlife. This life is a test; it is our opportunity to give our life to Jesus, to accept him as our personal Lord and Savior. Doing this is the only way to get to heaven. It is also our responsibility to try to save others and to spread the "good news." The primary responsibility of missionaries was to win over souls to Christ. Making life easier here on earth might be nice, but it was certainly more important to assure one's eternal life rather than one's very short earthly life.

I believed that the only way that God has spoken directly to us has been through the Bible. I was taught to believe in *Sola scriptura* (Scripture alone), a concept stressed particularly by Protestant Reformers such as Martin Luther. Although it may not have been expressed this way, we were taught to worship the Bible. It was suggested not to place anything on top of our Bibles such as other books. We had no education about where the Bible came from or how it came to be, but we were taught that it was the one and only word of God. We were taught that the Bible was without error and literally came directly from God.

I believed the Bible explained to us the origins of the world. The reason that it was created was for human beings. God created an earthly paradise, and the first two inhabitants were Adam and Eve. Apparently they sinned in short order; they disobeyed God by eating of the tree of the knowledge of good and evil. They were expelled from paradise, the garden of Eden. This was known as the "original sin" and as a result humankind has been flawed since. Mankind at its core is "evil." Adam and Eve had progeny, and the world continued in its evilness until God had had enough and sent a great flood to destroy everything with the exception of Noah and his family and a pair of each living creature. The world was to begin anew.

I was taught that after the great flood the history of mankind started over. The earth repopulated. Eventually God chose one man, Abraham, to be the "father" of a chosen people in a chosen land. Abraham's offspring grew in number and eventually became a people in bondage in the land of Egypt. A great leader, Moses, was chosen to lead the people out of bondage. Eventually the people came to populate the chosen land, the land of Israel. A great nation developed (Israel) although eventually it was conquered and eventually vanished. Prophets foretold that a messiah would be coming in the future who would restore Israel to glory. That messiah, when he came, was different than expected. Instead of coming as a conquering hero, Jesus was crucified on a cross by the Romans! However, he conquered death by being resurrected. He is the one and only son of God—in fact is God. He died as a sacrifice for the sins of mankind. In order to attain eternal life in heaven, all one needs to do is accept this fact and to accept Jesus as one's Lord and Savior. The Bible is God's revelation explaining all of this.

While growing up, it was my understanding that God had personal conversations with these early biblical figures. Just as two individuals have conversations together today, God had conversations with Adam and Eve, Noah, Abraham, and Moses. After the biblical period, God just stopped having such conversations with humans. The religion of Judaism was shaped directly from God. Although some of the Israelites strayed from the worship of Yahweh and worshiped other gods, Yahweh's way was clear and unchanging. Judaism was the religion taught by God. When Jesus came, this was a continuation of God's plan. Many followed the way of Jesus as God intended, but others rejected Jesus, the Messiah. In fact, many Jews were responsible for his death. My belief growing up was that Christianity was God's new testament, and that early Christians were unanimous in regards to Christ's teachings and what the essence of Christianity was. Judaism and later Christianity were monolithic religions.

I was taught that evil and sin were for the most part synonymous. All are sinful. All from time to time do evil. Although because of original sin we are inherently evil, we are also tempted to do evil by Satan, God's archenemy. God and Satan are in a cosmic battle between good and evil. Satan, the devil, abides in hell. He wants us to reject Jesus and God and to do what is evil. Then when we die we will be under his jurisdiction in hell forever and ever. Sin is basically doing what God has commanded us not to do or not doing what God has commanded us to do. There does not have to be a rhyme or reason to it, and we don't need to understand the reasons why. Ours is but to follow God's commands. For example, we might not know why God commanded Adam and Eve not to eat of a certain tree; we must obey God: "For my thoughts are not your thoughts, nor are your ways my ways, says the Lord. For as the heavens are higher than the earth, so are my ways higher than your ways and my thoughts than your thoughts" (Isa. 55:8–9).

Again, this is a summary of my worldview in my childhood. My worldview has changed, as reflected in the Postface of this book.

This present book is a summary of what I've learned about the origin of the Bible. Future proposed books deal with the following topics:

2. **Evolution of Religion**
   This book describes the evolution of religions, particularly Judaism and Christianity, and how they were influenced by other cultures (e.g., Egyptian, Mesopotamian, Persian, Greek, Roman, etc.).

3. **Evolution of Good and Evil**
   This book explores various conceptions of good and evil through the ages and currently. In particular, it describes the history of the development of Satan. It also explores commonalities between religions in regards to conceptions of goodness and evil.

4. **Evolution of the Universe**
   This book is a summary of what science tells us about the nature of things and the effects that information has on worldviews and belief in God. It deals with "big history," that is, getting a sense of the "big picture."

5. **Evolution of People and Culture**
   This book deals with developmental psychology, particularly cognitive development, moral development, and spiritual development. The book also deals with cultural development.

6. **Evolution of Church**
   This book explores the purposes of church for progressive Christians.

7. **Evolution of Spirituality**

This book focuses on advanced issues in spirituality, including the integration of all human knowledge into a coherent view of the universe.

I recommend two ways of reading this book. The first way would be to read the book in the typical fashion from cover to cover. A second way might be to skip to the Postface to see how my thoughts about the Bible have changed. Then in reading the content of this book one can see the information that was learned that changed my conceptions of the Bible.

Introduction

I was brought up believing that the Bible just somehow appeared from God, and this was the sum total of all that God had said to us. It happened thousands of years ago, and God has not spoken to us since in such a direct way. I was brought up to believe that every word of the Bible came directly from God. The real story is interesting, and much more complicated.

There appears to be a great ignorance in the United States about the Bible. Albert Mohler, president of the Southern Baptist Theological Seminary, wrote an article for Christianity.com in 2004 in which he bemoaned biblical illiteracy. "Researchers George Gallup and Jim Castelli put the problem squarely: 'Americans revere the Bible—but, by and large, they don't read it. And because they don't read it, they have become a nation of biblical illiterates.'" Dr. Mohler states:

- Fewer than half of all adults can name the four gospels.
- Sixty percent of Americans can't name even five of the ten commandments.
- According to 82% of Americans, "God helps those who help themselves," is a Bible verse.
- A majority of adults think the Bible teaches that the most important purpose in life is taking care of one's family.
- At least 12% of adults believe that Joan of Arc was Noah's wife.
- Over 50% of graduating high school seniors thought that Sodom and Gomorrah were husband and wife.
- A considerable number of respondents to one poll indicated that the Sermon on the Mount was preached by Billy Graham.

Dr. Mohler rightly advocates that people should read the Bible more and become knowledgeable about what's in it. However, I strongly believe that even though one could be intimately familiar with the content of the Bible and perhaps even have much of the Bible memorized, one could still be grossly ignorant about it. Every bit as important is knowledge about who wrote the various books that are in the Bible, what was the historical context, who decided what should be in the "canon," why there are differences between canons, etc.

One analogy might be knowledge about a historic home. I live in a district of historic homes, and every year there is a tour of six or seven of these homes. There are tour guides at each of the homes giving information about the houses. I would feel very deprived if during one of these tours I was only given information such as how many steps there are in the front staircase, how many fireplaces there are in the home, the colors of the paint on the walls, the types of wood that are used on the hardwood floors, etc. More interesting would be information such as when the house was built, who built it, the style of architecture, dates of additions, history of owners, what was the neighborhood like when it was built, etc. And so it is with the Bible. To really know and understand it, we must study other sources that give us information about its historical context.

The Bible is not a single book. It is a collection of writings that in the case of the Christian Bible was written over a 1,500-year period starting in the Bronze Age and continuing into the Hellenistic-Roman Period.

Biblical Periods

The time period purported to be covered by the books of the Bible (both Old and New Testaments) can be broken down into sections. It is important to keep in mind these historical periods when interpreting content of the various books. In this book we will examine each of the books of the Old and New Testaments within their historical contexts and also in the historical periods in which they were believed to have been written.

- 4000 to 2000 B.C.E.   The Primeval Period
- 2000 to 1700 B.C.E.   The Patriarchal Period
- 1700 to 1200 B.C.E.   The Egyptian Period
- 1200 to 1000 B.C.E.   The Tribal Period
- 1000 to 900 B.C.E.   The Davidic Kingdom
- 900 to 600 B.C.E.   The Divided Kingdoms
- 600 to 540 B.C.E.   The Babylonian Period
- 540 to 330 B.C.E.   The Persian Period
- 330 to 170 B.C.E.   The Greek Period
- 170 to 63 B.C.E.   The Maccabean Period
- 63 B.C.E. to 150 C.E.   The Roman Period

B.C.E. stands for "before the Common Era," and C.E. refers to the "Common Era." These terms have generally replaced B.C. and A.D., which stood for "before Christ" and *anno domini* (Latin for "year of our Lord"), respectively.

The Periods in Which Books of the Hebrew Bible Were Written

Divided Kingdoms	Babylonian Period	Persian Period	Greek Period
Ruth	Lamentations	1, 2 Chronicles	Ecclesiastes
Genesis	Ezekiel	Ezra	Song of Solomon
Exodus		Nehemiah	Daniel
Leviticus		Esther	1, 2 Maccabees
Numbers		Job	Tobit
Deuteronomy		Psalms	Judith
Joshua		Proverbs	Susanna
Judges		Joel	Bel and the Dragon
1, 2 Samuel		Obadiah	Wisdom of Solomon
1, 2 Kings		Jonah	Wisdom of Ben Sira
Isaiah		Haggai	Enoch
Jeremiah		Zechariah	Jubilees
Hosea		Malachi	
Amos			
Micah			
Nahum			
Habakkuk			
Zephaniah			

Chapter 1

Before the Bible Was Written

Timeline of Important Events

2100 B.C.E.	Epic of Gilgamesh
1800–1700	Patriarchs
1750	Code of Hammurabi
1700–1300	Israel in Egypt
1300	Exodus from Egypt
1250–1200	The "conquest"
1200–1000	Period of the Judges
1000–922	Davidic Monarchy
	Time of the hypothetical "J" writer

The Primeval Period
(4,000 to 2,000 B.C.E.)

The term "primeval" refers to the earliest, most ancient ages in human history. This era is covered in the book of Genesis and includes the stories of creation, the beginnings of sin, the great flood, and the Tower of Babel and the confusion of languages. However, the book of Genesis was not written during this era and was written much later.

There was a writing, however, which may have been written during this period. It is called "The Epic of Gilgamesh" and it may have been written as early as 2100 B.C.E. It was written in Akkadian, the Babylonian language. A fragment, dated to 1550–1150 B.C.E. has been found during excavations at Megiddo, which is located in northern Israel. The early Hebrew people likely had exposure to this epic. This is one of the earliest surviving pieces of literature that we have in existence.

There is a story of creation in the Epic of Gilgamesh which parallels the Genesis creation stories. In the epic a man (Enkidu) is created from the soil by a god. He lives in a natural setting amongst the animals. He gets introduced to a woman who tempts him. Like the Genesis story, he accepts food from the woman, covers his nakedness, and must leave this former realm never to be able to return. Later in this epic a snake steals a plant of immortality from the hero (Gilgamesh).

There also is a flood story in the Epic of Gilgamesh. Flood stories were widespread in the ancient Near East, and it is highly likely that versions of a flood story were written centuries before biblical Israel existed. Although this was a widespread story in the ancient Near East, there is no archaeological or geological evidence that a worldwide flood ever happened.

In Genesis there is evidence of two different sources contributing to the flood story, and passages from the two sources appear to be combined together, i.e., passage from one source, followed by a passage from the other source, followed by the first source again, etc. The first source (known as "J" and explained later in this book) uses the name "Yahweh" to describe God. In the J narrative, God instructs Noah to bring into the ark, which he is instructed to build, seven pairs of the clean animals and birds and two pairs of the unclean animals. The flood lasts 40 days. After the flood, Noah releases three doves in succession; when the third did not return, he knew there was dry land. He then built an altar and sacrificed some of the clean animals and birds to God.

The other source for the flood narrative is known as "P" (and again will be explained later in this book). "P" uses the name Elohim to describe God. In his version, God tells Noah to bring in one pair of each type of animal (a male and a female). While in "J" the flood is caused by rain, in "P" it results from an undoing of nature. According to "P" the flood lasts for a year, not the 40 days of "J." In "P" Noah releases a raven, not the three doves as in "J." With "P" there is no sacrifice to God (with only one pair of each animal, there are none to spare!).

There are close parallels between biblical and non-biblical accounts of the flood. In both accounts there is godly anger and the hero of the story is warned about an upcoming flood with detailed instructions about how to build a boat that will house his family and animals. After the flood the boat rests on the top of a mountain, and birds are released (in Gilgamesh, it is three doves).

The Patriarchal Period
(2,000 to 1,700 B.C.E.)

Also in the book of Genesis is the narrative of the patriarchal fathers. These are the stories of Abram and Sarai, their journey from Ur of the Chaldeans to the land of Canaan, the births of Ishmael and Isaac, the beginnings of circumcision, doom of Sodom and Gomorrah, the births of Jacob and Esau, God changing Jacob's name to Israel, Joseph's successes in Egypt, and the descendants of Israel moving to Egypt due to famine. No biblical books were written during this period, and these stories were handed down orally.

The three patriarchs are all very different. Abraham is a paragon of virtue and is unquestionably obedient. Isaac is not a very well developed character. Jacob is complex and sometimes treacherous. Nowhere in the non-biblical records of that time, however, can mention be found of Abraham, Isaac, Jacob, or Joseph. Conversely, in Genesis no known historical figures of that time are mentioned. Genesis is vague and never mentions by name the pharaohs that Abraham and Joseph interacted with. This leads many scholars to believe that the patriarchs were not historical figures. Many scholars believe these stories were folklore developed to raise issues of morality, theology, and community identity. Not only do these stories provide an explanation for the origin of the Jewish people, they also give an explanation for the origin of the other heathen cultures of the area. The Edomites are the descendants of

Esau. The Moabites are the descendants of the incestuous relationship between Lot and his daughter. The Ammonites are descendants of the incestuous relationship between Lot and another daughter.

The Egyptian Period
(1700 to 1200 B.C.E.)

The book of Exodus says that the people of Israel greatly multiplied in Egypt where they lived for many years. The pharaoh, the king of Egypt, became concerned about their growth and ordered that all of the Israelite male infants be killed. Actually, it is only in the Greek version of Exodus, the Septuagint, that it is stated that Hebrew male infants should be put to death. In the earlier Hebrew version of Exodus it says that *all* male infants should be put to death. As in Genesis, the name of the pharaoh is not given, and there is no mention in Egyptian writings of this event ever occurring. Even though all of the males of Moses's generation were supposedly killed, during the Exodus there does not appear to be a shortage of males of that age (including Aaron who is three years older than Moses).

The story of Moses's infancy parallels the story of Sargon the Great, Mesopotamian emperor (23rd to 22nd centuries B.C.E.). Sargon's mother was a priestess who secretly conceived him, set him in a basket of reeds, and cast him into the river. Akki, "the drawer of water," rescued him and raised him as his son. Rescue narratives of important political and religious leaders were common in ancient cultures, and other examples include Dionysus, Heracles, Oedipus, Cyrus, Zarathustra in Persia, Romulus in Rome, and Jesus.

In Exodus 3, God appears to Moses in the form of a burning bush. God wants Moses to lead the people of Israel out of Egyptian bondage, but Moses is very reluctant. Such reluctance is also a common theme in this time period for prophets and leaders, e.g., Jeremiah and Gideon. Moses finally agrees to lead the Israelites with Aaron as his right-hand man and spokesperson. It is Aaron's job to tell the pharaoh to let the Israelites go, but for some reason God intentionally "hardens" the pharaoh's heart. Aaron is to perform a wonder; he throws down his staff which turns into a snake. Pharaoh's magicians are able to replicate this wonder, however. It is then that God sends 10 plagues. The first two plagues were replicated by pharaoh's magicians. After each plague pharaoh agrees to free the Israelites, but then has a "change of heart." These are the 10 plagues:

1. The water of the Nile River turns to blood.
2. Swarm of frogs
3. Swarm of gnats
4. Swarm of flies
5. Deadly pestilence of livestock (horses, donkeys, camels, herds, flocks)
6. Festering boils on humans and livestock
7. Heavy hail
8. Swarm of locusts
9. Three days of heavy darkness
10. The firstborn of every Egyptian and livestock are killed.

Pharaoh finally relents, but then, once again, he changes his mind and pursues the Israelites. It is then that we have the famous story of the Red Sea opening up to let the Israelites cross and then crashing in on the pursuing Egyptians. The

Hebrew term for the body of water that was crossed is *yam suf* which literally means "sea of reeds." It was the Greek version of Scripture, the Septuagint, that translated this as the Red Sea rather than the Reed Sea. This may explain the miracle; the Israelites escaped through the marshes, and the Egyptian chariots got stuck in the mud.

There is no mention in the considerable writings of Egypt of any of this ever occurring—no mention of Moses, Aaron, the Hebrews, the plagues, or a defeat at sea. This leads some skeptics to believe that the Exodus never occurred. Most scholars, however, do believe that some type of exodus did occur, although much of the story has been aggrandized. The date of the exodus is uncertain, but the time period between the 16th and the 13th centuries B.C.E. has been proposed).

The Israelites journey to Mount Sinai. This is where God gives the Ten Commandments to Moses. It is at Sinai that God said he was going to make a covenant with the Israelites; they were to be his "treasured possession out of all the peoples" and would be a "priestly kingdom and a holy nation." First God made a covenant with Noah (no more floods), then with Abraham (his descendants would be a great nation in a promised land), and now with the Israelite people. The Noahic covenant was between God and all people of the earth. The other two covenants were between God and specific groups of people, descendants of Abraham, and then the Israelites.

The Ten Commandments are a contract between Yahweh and Israel. In order for the Israelites to be God's special people, there are rules and requirements they must keep. Not only are the commandments addressed specifically to the Israelite people (and not the other peoples of the world), they are addressed to individual Israelite males, the only really important people in this patriarchal society. The commandments are phrased in the second-person, masculine singular. The first four commandments have to do with the relationship between Yahweh and the Israelites:

1. Israelites are not to worship other gods. It is not that there aren't other gods; it is just that as part of this contract the Israelites must exclusively worship Yahweh.
2. The Israelites were forbidden from making images of Yahweh, a practice common in this time period. This sets Yahweh apart from the other gods in this respect.
3. The name of Yahweh should be used properly and respectfully (the name "Yahweh" God was hesitant to give at all in Exod. 3:13–15, and Jews in post-biblical times often avoided saying the name aloud).
4. Keep the Sabbath day holy. This is to emulate God who rested on the seventh day after completing creation and also for humanitarian reasons, e.g., giving one's slaves a break.

The remaining six commandments have to do with keeping order in the Israelite community:

5. Honor your father and mother.
6. Don't murder.
7. Don't commit adultery.
8. Don't steal.
9. Don't bear false witness against your neighbor.
10. Don't covet your neighbor's house, wife, slave, livestock, or any belongings of your neighbor.

The Ten Commandments or "Decalogue" has been summarized as love and exclusive worship of Yahweh as well as love for one's neighbors (other Israelites).

The rest of Exodus and the book of Leviticus have to do with more laws and rituals for the Israelite people. The most important of these codes are the Covenant Code in Exodus, the Holiness Code in Leviticus, and the Deuteronomic Code in Deuteronomy. Such collections of laws and codes were common in the ancient Near East, and one of the earliest that have been discovered is the Code of Hammurabi, dating to the first half of the 18th century B.C.E. and predating the Israelite laws and codes. The code contains nearly three hundred laws that outline in detail what the punishment should be if certain laws are broken. These same types of laws are included in the book of Exodus, e.g., "When an ox gores a man or a woman to death, the ox shall be stoned, and its flesh shall not be eaten; but the owner of the ox shall not be liable" (Exod. 21:28). There also are laws about slavery, e.g.: "When a slaveowner strikes a male or female slave with a rod and the slave dies immediately, the owner shall be punished. But if the slave survives a day or two, there is no punishment; for the slave is the owner's property" (Exod. 21:20–21).

The book of Leviticus also gives detailed instructions about the construction of the ark of the covenant, construction of the Tabernacle, and detailed instructions about priestly vestments. Leviticus gives detailed instructions on how and when to make sacrifices, the rites of ordination, what are "clean" and "unclean" food, purification issues (e.g., menstruation, leprosy), sexual laws, and instructions about festivals. Chapters 17–26 of Leviticus are known as the Holiness Code. To be holy is to be separate from the impure, such as the other peoples the Israelites have been in contact with (Egyptians, Canaanites). God wants them to be separate. They have laws, including dietary laws, which separate them from the impure nations. Circumcision separates the Israelites from others. All of these laws were not written for mankind; they were written for the Israelite people to separate them from other peoples.

The book of Numbers has a variety of different types of materials within it. It includes a census of all the Israelites (hence it's name of "Numbers"), instructions about the order of the camp, more writings about laws and regulations (for the most part duplicates of laws given in Exodus and Leviticus), instructions about inheritance for those with no male descendants, regulations for the Nazirites (men and women who take a special vow to separate themselves to the Lord—they abstain from alcohol, don't cut their hair, and they don't go near corpses), information about the Levites, narratives about the continuing journey from Egypt to Canaan, descriptions of rebellions of the people against Moses and Yahweh, wandering in the wilderness for 40 years, military encounters with other peoples, the appointing of Joshua as Moses' successor, and another census.

The book of Deuteronomy contains little narrative but is mostly a speech given by Moses prior to his death. It is written in third person, i.e., "These are the words that Moses spoke." According to 2 Kings, during repairs in the temple in Jerusalem during the reign of King Josiah, a scroll was found —the book of Deuteronomy. Inspired by the book, Josiah implemented a number of reforms in the country which included destroying all shrines to other gods and presiding over a national celebration of Passover.

In Deuteronomy Moses gives the great commandment "You shall love the Lord your God with all your heart, and with all your soul, and with all your might." The Deuteronomic Code includes directions to destroy pagan shrines, directions for worship, dietary regulations, and criminal and civil laws. The book ends describing the death and burial of Moses.

It should be kept in mind that all of the laws and regulations outlined in the Torah are specifically meant for the Israelite people to distinguish them from other peoples in the area. The same goes for circumcision. Again, God is not giving these laws for all of humanity; they are meant for the Israelites.

The book of Deuteronomy is considered the fifth and final book of the Torah, but it also has been proposed to be the theological preface to another group of writings known as the "Deuteronomistic History" which includes the books of Joshua, Judges, Samuel, and Kings. This group of books continues the history of the Israelite people from where the Torah leaves off until the Babylonian captivity.

On the other hand, it has also been proposed that the book of Joshua is a continuation of the Pentateuch (i.e., perhaps we should think of a "Hexateuch") as it appears that all six of these books were a conglomeration of writings from J, E, D, and P (the "Documentary Hypothesis" will be explained later in this book).

In the book of Joshua, the character Joshua is now leading the Israelites across the Jordan to capture Canaan, the "Promised Land." In the famous "Battle of Jericho," God told Joshua to have the Israelites march around the city daily for six days, and then on the 7th day to march around it seven times, with the priests blowing the ram's horn. The people shouted, the walls "came tumblin' down" (according to the well-known spiritual), the Israelites charged in and then killed every man, woman, child and animal.

In some passages of the book of Joshua it appears that the Israelites have completely defeated all of the native peoples in Canaan, and this act of genocide was purportedly God's will. In other parts of the book of Joshua, however, and in the book of Judges, it appears that the "conquest" was actually incomplete. Joshua divides the lands between the 12 Tribes. The book of Joshua presents the people of Israel as united together and united in their worship of Yahweh.

Although these six books describe events of these time periods, the books were actually written much later. Stories were passed down orally from one generation to another until eventually people started writing the stories down.

The Tribal Period
(1200 to 1000 B.C.E.)

The book of Judges presents us with a very different vision of the people of Israel than did the book of Joshua. Here the Israelites repeatedly are in conflict with each other and they continually worship other gods. The pattern during this period is of repeated apostasy followed by repeated punishments by God for this. The people of Israel coexisted during this time with the Canaanites, who it turns out were not conquered. The Israelites during this time period were led by "judges" who were not judges in the modern sense of the term but were, rather, military leaders. Although the book of Judges would suggest that the various judges were in power sequentially, this is not likely as the combined years would total more than four centuries, rather than the two centuries that would be expected. More than likely these judges were local leaders and that there were overlapping "judgings." Scholars divided the judges into two groups: the major judges that the book describes in some detail (Othniel, Ehud, Shamgar, Deborah, Gideon, Jephthah, and Samson), and the minor judges who are not described much at all (Tolah, Jair, Ibzan, Elon, and Abdon).

One of the judges, Deborah, was a woman, and it is noteworthy that the biblical writers do not seem to think that this is remarkable and present her role as judge, prophet, and military leader quite matter-of-factly. The last judge, Samson, was the most famous. He was a Nazirite—a group of people mentioned earlier that refrained from alcohol and cutting of their hair. He had great strength and was a Herculean character. His major flaw was foreign women. One of these, Delilah, a likely Philistine, cut his hair while he was sleeping. He lost his strength and was seized by the Philistines who gouged his eyes out. He was put in prison, and then his hair began growing back. His final act was a show of strength. He pushed over pillars, killing himself and three thousand Philistine men and women.

It would appear that in this two-century period the Israelites were a loosely knit union of tribes, and in many respects the Israelite people were impossible to tell apart from the Canaanites living in the area. What did distinguish the Israelite tribes was the "covenant" to only worship Yahweh and to provide mutual support and defense for each other. The Israelites and the Canaanites were of the same culture and all were descents of Abraham. According to legend only the Israelites were descendants of Jacob, however. The group intermingled, and there were intermarriages. Not only did the Israelite people at times worship pagan gods, but also some Canaanite people joined the Israelites and worshipped Yahweh.

The book of Ruth is set "in the days when the judges ruled." The book is historical fiction. It tells the story of Ruth, a widowed Moabite, and her mother-in-law, Naomi, an Israelite who is also widowed. The two plot to get Ruth married to a wealthy man so that each can then receive financial support and protection. The significance of the story is that Ruth is the great-grandmother of David, future king of Israel.

The Davidic Kingdom
(1000 to 900 B.C.E.)

This period of Israelite history is covered in the books of 1 and 2 Samuel and 1 and 2 Kings. First and Second Samuel was originally one book. Samuel is a prophet who was born to Hannah, who like so many mothers in the Bible of very special sons, had trouble conceiving but eventually does become pregnant as the result of prayer. Samuel is a priest, prophet and judge and is very much in God's favor. The people of Israel request a king like other peoples in that geographical area, and Samuel (and God) reluctantly relents. There became more of a necessity for a centralized government and a professional army due to threats of the Philistines in the area. Saul, a military leader, was anointed by Samuel as Israel's first king. In regards to Saul, "There was not a man among the people of Israel more handsome than he; he stood head and shoulders above everyone else" (1 Sam. 9:2).

Saul has a number of successful military victories. God tells him to totally destroy the Amalekites: "Now go and attack Amalek, and utterly destroy all that they have; do not spare them, but kill both man and woman, child and infant, ox and sheep, camel and donkey" (1 Sam. 15:3). Saul, however, spared their king, Agag, and "the best of the sheep and of the cattle and of the fatlings, and the lambs, and all that was valuable." God was angry at this: "I regret that I made Saul king, for he has turned back from following me." God decides there should be a new king. Samuel meets David: "he was ruddy, and had beautiful eyes, and was handsome. The Lord said, 'Rise and anoint him; for this is the one'" (1 Sam. 16:12).

David's anointing as king was a secret. David becomes a servant in Saul's court and comes to be loved by Saul. David marries one of Saul's daughters and becomes close friends with Saul's son, Jonathan. First Samuel contains the story of David killing the great Philistine giant, Goliath, although in 2 Samuel that same Goliath is said to have been killed by Elhanan, son of Jaare-oregim. David's popularity grows, and Saul comes to see him as a threat and so seeks to kill him. David flees to southern Judah. Saul and his son, Jonathan, are later killed in battle.

David learns of Saul's death and is chosen to be king of the tribe of Judah. Saul's son, Ishbaal, is the king of the northern tribes, but after he is assassinated David is accepted as the king of the northern tribes as well. David makes Jerusalem the capital of the kingdom, and he moves the ark of the covenant there. This is the beginning of a golden age of a unified kingdom, but the story of King David is not completely glorious, and David is not completely virtuous. On the positive, he is able to defeat the enemies of Israel, including the Philistines. He is a poet, a musician, and a gifted warrior. On the negative side, he has an affair with Bathsheba, whom he gets pregnant, and then he arranges for Bathsheba's husband to be killed. David had 17 sons by various wives. His third-born, Absalom, rebelled against David and attempted to take the throne. When David was dying the heir apparent was David's son, Adonijah, who attempted to have himself crowned as king. Bathsheba convinced David to instead crown her son, Solomon, as king.

Solomon is anointed king by the prophet Nathan and the priest Zadok. Although Solomon's reign is known for his wisdom and piety, his early acts were to ruthlessly eliminate all of his rivals, including his half-brother Adonijah. A major accomplishment of Solomon was to build a temple to God in Jerusalem. This would be the home of the ark of the covenant and of God. Solomon had tremendous wealth, and much of this was due to a very heavily taxed peasantry. Although this was known as a "golden age," it likely was not for all. Solomon's vast wealth included 700 wives and 300 concubines. Such wealth was seen in those times to suggest God's favor. The theology of that time was that evil was punished, and good was rewarded. Although numerous wives and concubines were not seen as evil, having foreign wives was. This got Solomon into trouble; "for when Solomon was old, his wives turned away his heart after other gods; and his heart was not true to the Lord his God" (1 Kings 11:4). As a result, God said that he would tear the kingdom of Israel from his son.

Other than in the books of the Bible, there is no other outside corroboration for the lives of Saul, David, and Solomon.

Chapter 2

Writing the Old Testament

Timeline of Important Events

922–722	The Divided Kingdom
	Time of the hypothetical "E" writer
850	Elijah
c. 750	Amos
c. 740	Hosea
722	Assyrian conquest of Israel; dispersal of the 10 northern tribes
715–687	Hezekiah rules the Southern Kingdom
700	The first Isaiah
640–609	Josiah
622	Josiah finds the Book of Deuteronomy and implements Deuteronomic Reforms
612	Nineveh (Assyrian capital) falls to Babylon
609	Josiah is killed and the Deuteronomic Reform ends
c. 620–597	Jeremiah
597	First deportation to Babylon
587	Nebuchadnezzar destroys Jerusalem; second deportation; Solomon's temple is destroyed.
587–539	Ezekiel; the second Isaiah; the priestly writers edit J and E
522–486	Work on rebuilding the temple begins
465–424	Ezra
423	Nehemiah
331	Alexander the Great conquers the Persian Empire

The Divided Kingdoms
(900 to 600 B.C.E.)

After Solomon's death, he was succeeded by his son Rehoboam. Because Rehoboam refused to give the people tax relief, the northern tribes seceded, and Jeroboam was made their king. Because the temple in Jerusalem in the south was where people made sacrifices to God, Jeroboam needed to replace this in the northern kingdom so that people would not travel south to Jerusalem. He built two calves of gold and placed one in Bethel in the southern part of his kingdom and one in Dan in the northern part of the kingdom. These were shrines for the people to worship. He also appointed new priests, who were not from the tribe of Levi. The books of 1 and 2 Kings describe the succession of kings in both kingdoms. In discussing each of the kings, the author takes special interest in whether or not they were faithful in following the laws of God, particularly whether they worshiped only him or turned to false gods. I have put in bold font all of the kings that were perceived as righteous. As you will see, none of the kings of the northern kingdom of Israel were presented this way. Judah was mixed: Some kings were righteous, and some were evil. The quotations are the Bible's descriptions of each of the kings.

The Northern Kingdom of Israel

- Jeroboam I (922–901 B.C.E.). He "did not turn from his evil way."
- Nadab (901–900). This is Jeroboam's son. "He did what was evil in the sight of the Lord."
- Baasha (900–877). "He did what was evil in the sight of the Lord."

- Elah (877–876). Because of all the sins that he and his father, Baasha, committed with idols, the house of Baasha was destroyed.

- Zimri (876). When Elah was drunk, he was murdered by Zimri who then also killed the entire house of Baasha. Zimri was king only seven days. Omri, the commander of the army, besieged the town that Zimri was in to avenge King Elah's death. Zimri died in a fire "because of the sins that he committed, doing evil in the sight of the Lord."

- Omri (876–869). "Omri did what was evil in the sight of the Lord; he did more evil than all who were before him."

- Ahab (869–850). "Ahab son of Omri did evil in the sight of the Lord more than all who were before him." Ahab served and worshiped Baal.

- Ahaziah (850–849). "He did what was evil in the sight of the Lord."

- Jehoram (849–843/2). Because Ahaziah had no son, his brother, Jehoram, succeeded him. "He did what was evil in the sight of the Lord."

- Jehu (843/2–815). The story of Jehu is an interesting one. He was supported for king by the prophet, Elisha. He murdered both King Jehoram of Israel and King Ahaziah of Judah who were related to each other. He had Jehoram's mother, Jezebel, thrown from a window. Jehu drove his chariot over her body, which later was eaten by dogs. He had all 70 of Ahab's son's killed. He then slaughtered 42 relatives of King Ahaziah. Once in control in Samaria he killed the worshippers of Baal, destroyed their temple, and banned the worship of Baal. God was apparently happy with this: "you have done well in carrying out what I consider right," "Although

Jehu was not careful to follow the law of the Lord the God of Israel with all his heart."

- Jehoahaz (815–802). This is the son of Jehu. "He did what was evil in the sight of the Lord."
- Jehoash (802–786). "He also did what was evil in the sight of the Lord."
- Jeroboam II (786–746). "He did what was evil in the sight of the Lord."
- Zechariah (746–745). "He did what was evil in the sight of the Lord."
- Shallum (745). Shallum reigned for only one month until he was assassinated by Menahem.
- Menahem (745–737). "He did what was evil in the sight of the Lord."
- Pekahiah (737–736). "He did what was evil in the sight of the Lord."
- Pekah (736–732). "He did what was evil in the sight of the Lord."
- Hoshea (732–724). "He did what was evil in the sight of the Lord."

The fall of Samaria occurred in 722 B.C.E.. The powerful Assyrian Empire led by Shalmaneser V and later his successor and brother, Sargon II, besieged Samaria, the capital of Israel's northern kingdom, and made the northern kingdom an Assyrian province. It was the practice of the Assyrians to send conquered peoples to other lands and then to repopulate the territories conquered with people from other conquered territories. Dispersing nations diminished the chances of national uprisings to occur. The northern kingdom of Israel would never be heard from again. These would be the 10 lost tribes of Israel (tribes of Reuben, Issachar, Zebulun, Dan, Naphtali, Gad, Asher, Ephraim, and

Manasseh). The tribes of Judah and Benjamin are what formed the Kingdom of Judah.

The reason for the Assyrian conquest of the northern kingdom is clear in the second book of Kings. "This occurred because the people of Israel had sinned against the Lord their God, who had brought them up out of the land of Egypt from under the hand of pharaoh, king of Egypt. They had worshiped other gods and walked in the customs of the nations whom the Lord drove out before the people of Israel, and in the customs that the kings of Israel had introduced" (2 Kings 17:7–8).

The Southern Kingdom of Judah

Judah fared better than did Israel. Whereas Israel fell to the Assyrians in 722 B.C.E., Judah continued as a nation until they were conquered by the Babylonians in 598 B.C.E. (124 years later). All of the kings of Israel were perceived as doing "evil in the sight of the Lord," but some of the kings of Judah were perceived as doing "what was right in the sight of the Lord."

- Rehoboam (922–915 B.C.E.). This is Solomon's son, and he is presented in a negative light. The people of Judah are said to have done "evil in the sight of the Lord" "more than all that their ancestors had done."
- Abijam (915–913). "He committed all the sins that his father did before him; his heart was not true to the Lord his God."
- **Asa (913–873). "Asa did what was right in the sight of the Lord."**

- **Jehoshaphat (873–849). "He walked in all the way of his father Asa; he did not turn aside from it, doing what was right in the sight of the Lord."**
- Jehoram (849–843/2). "He did what was evil in the sight of the Lord."
- Ahaziah (843/2). "He also walked in the way of the house of Ahab, doing what was evil in the sight of the Lord." He was murdered by Jehu.
- Athaliah (843/2–837). This is the mother of Ahaziah. She sought to kill all of the rest of the royal family, although Ahaziah's infant son was hidden away. At the age of 7, Johoash, Ahaziah's son, appeared. Athaliah was put to death.
- **Jehoash (837–800). Began his reign at the age of seven after his grandmother, Athaliah, was put to death. "Johoash did what was right in the sight of the Lord all his days."**
- **Amaziah (800–783). "He did what was right in the sight of the Lord."**
- **Azariah/Uzziah (783–742). "He did what was right in the sight of the Lord."**
- **Jotham (742–735). "He did what was right in the sight of the Lord."**
- Ahaz (735–715). "He did not do what was right in the sight of the Lord his God."
- **Hezekiah (715–687/6). "He did what was right in the sight of the Lord." "He removed the high places, broke down the pillars, and cut down the sacred pole. He broke in pieces the bronze serpent that Moses had made, for until those days the people of Israel had made offerings to it; it was called Nehushtan. He trusted in the Lord the God of Israel; so that there was no one like him**

among all the kings of Judah after him, or among those who were before him.”

- Manasseh (687/6–642). “He did what was evil in the sight of the Lord.”
- Amon (642–640). “He did what was evil in the sight of the Lord.”
- **Josiah (640–609). “He did what was right in the sight of the Lord.”**
- Jehoahaz (609). “He did what was evil in the sight of the Lord.”
- Jehoiakim (609–598). “He did what was evil in the sight of the Lord.”
- Jehoiachin (598/7). Jehoiachin began his reign at the age of 18. “He did what was evil in the sight of the Lord.” King Nebuchadnezzar of Babylon came to Jerusalem, and the city was besieged. King Jehoiachin was imprisoned. The king’s house and Solomon’s temple was looted. Ten thousand citizens of Judah (warriors, officials, artisans, and smiths) were brought to Babylon. Only poor people were left in the land.
- Zedekiah (597–587/6). The king of Babylon made Mattaniah, Jehoiachin’s uncle, king and changed his name to Zedekiah. “He did what was evil in the sight of the Lord.”

Zedekiah ended up rebelling against the king of Babylon, and so Nebuchadnezzar and his army again came to Jerusalem in 587. The city fell, and King Zedekiah was captured and taken prisoner to Babylon. More of the elite citizens of Judah were deported to Babylon as well. Solomon’s temple was destroyed.

Documentary Hypothesis

It is during the periods of the divided kingdoms of Judah and Israel that the first books of the Bible were written. Most biblical scholars agree that Moses did not write the books of the Torah (**Genesis, Exodus, Leviticus, Numbers,** and **Deuteronomy**) . Many scholars believe there were five principal authors of these books. They are known as the Yahwist source (J), the Elohist source (E), the Deuteronomist (D), and the Priestly source (P). This was articulated as the "Documentary Hypothesis" by Julius Wellhausen (1844–1918), a German historian. It is called a "hypothesis" because we do not have any of these actual early manuscripts, and we only hypothesize that they existed. This is deduced because it is evident to biblical scholars that the style and content of various passages in these books are very different from each other. If you've ever read the Torah straight through you've probably noticed the many redundancies ("didn't I already read all this before?") and contradictions.

The earliest source is thought to be the Yahwist source (J). You may wonder why it is signified with a "J." The reason is that Yahweh is spelled in German as "Jahwe," hence a "J." The Yahwist wrote down stories that had been passed down orally for many generations. Likely the stories were much lengthier and involved in the oral traditions (there are allusions to other stories that are not explained or developed in J, for example in Gen. 6:4 "The Nephilim were on the earth in those day—and also afterward—when the sons of God went in to the daughters of humans, who bore children to them. These were the heroes of old, warriors of renown." Likely early readers would have known to what this was referring). Scholars believe J was written in the ninth or tenth centuries B.C.E. and originated in the area of the southern kingdom of Judah. God is called "Yahweh" and is very anthropomorphic. For example, he is able to walk in the garden of Eden and he enjoys "pleasing odors."

The other early source is the Elohist (E). God is called "Elohim" by this source, and it is believed to have originated in the northern part of Israel. Scholars believe it was written in the ninth or eighth centuries B.C.E. Elohim is much less anthropomorphic than the God of the Yahwist. Again, the material for the narratives of the Elohist come from generations of orally transmitted stories. Many scholars believe the J and E sources were combined in the seventh century after the fall of the northern kingdom.

The "P" or Priestly source emphasizes rituals and religious observances such as dietary laws, circumcision, and Sabbath observance. "P" concerns itself with genealogies. The God of "P" is even more remote and transcendent than the God of "E." Most of the Priestly source likely was written in the sixth century.

The last major source for writings in the Torah is the Deuteronomist (D). This writer is responsible for the content found in the book of Deuteronomy. Scholars believe the book likely originated in the northern kingdom of Israel. **Genesis, Exodus, Leviticus,** and **Numbers** were written primarily by "J," "E," and "P." **Deuteronomy** was written by the Deuteronomistic Historians.

Deuteronomistic Historians

Scholars believe that the books of **Deuteronomy, Joshua, Judges, 1-2 Samuel,** and **1-2 Kings** actually comprise a single literary unit. The other two great historical works in the Hebrew Bible are the Tetrateuch (Genesis through Numbers) and the Chronicles (1-2 Chronicles and Ezra-Nehemiah) which were written much later in history. Scholars believe that a later editor moved the story of the death of Moses from the end of Numbers to the end of Deuteronomy so that Deuteronomy would fit in better with the other four books, thus forming a "Pentateuch" rather than a "Tetrateuch."

It is not known whether the Deuteronomistic history was written by a single author/compiler, or if it was written by a group of writers who shared an ideology. The primary aim of the Deuteronomistic historian(s) was to show contemporaries during the time of the Babylonian exile that their sufferings were the result of centuries of not following Yahweh and the Deuteronomic law. God did not fail the Jewish people; the Jewish people failed God.

Although the Deuteronomistic History likely came together around 562 (after the fall of Judah), many who believe that it was written by a "school" rather than an individual think its beginnings may have been in the northern kingdom of Israel. Ancient traditions preserved by northern prophets came to the southern kingdom of Judah after Israel's fall. An early form of the book of Deuteronomy may have been written during Hezekiah's reign. During the reign of Josiah—approximately a half century later—a "book of the law" was discovered in the temple (2 Kings 22:8). Josiah used this to reform Judah. At this point the Deuteronomistic school was revived. There were additional writings over the years and editing. The final form of the Deuteronomistic History likely was during the Babylonian exile.

To summarize the history of the composition of the first 12 books of the Bible (Genesis through 2 Kings), the earliest two sources were the Yahwist (J) and the Elohist (E). Both combined centuries of oral traditions. The Yahwist was from the south and probably wrote in the ninth or 10th centuries. The Elohist was from the north and probably wrote in the eighth or ninth centuries. They were likely combined around 700 B.C.E. in the southern kingdom (after the fall of Israel in the north). The Priestly source (P) likely wrote in the sixth century. Not only did "P" write much of the material in the Pentateuch (especially instructions regarding religious rituals that were already in existence), but "P" also combined the writings of "J," "E," and "D" with his own writings to form what is now known as the Pentateuch. This would have happened around 550 B.C.E., after the fall of Judah and during the Babylonian captivity. This would have been necessary in order to preserve Jewish traditions while the Jews were removed from their homeland.

The earliest version of Deuteronomy may have been written during the reign of King Hezekiah in Judah (715–686), but the completed Deuteronomistic History likely was not written until the Babylonian exile, around the time of "P." There is some disagreement as to who finally redacted all of the writings: many would say "P," but others believe the Deuteronomists did the final redacting.

Although the book of Ruth in the Bible tells a story that occurs during the period of the Judges, it likely was not written until the Persian period.

Prophets

Prophets were common in the ancient Near East including with the Israelite people. They were known to be individuals who had special abilities that came from the divine. Their function was to relay messages from God, to be critics of society, and to predict the future. Divination involves practices to determine the will of God or gods. It was common in the ancient Near East and in Israel. One practice to determine God's will was the use of the *Urim* and *Thummim*, which was apparently like throwing dice to determine the will of God. Casting of lots was common for the Israelite people. Necromancy, consulting the dead, also was used. King Saul was able to conjure up the spirit of the dead prophet, Samuel, for consultation (1 Sam. 28:14).

Many prophets were trained professionals who made their living in this. The importance of prophets appears to correlate with the Israelite monarchies. Prophets are relatively rare prior to the monarchies (exceptions are Abraham and Moses) and after the monarchies. Samuel is an important prophet during the reign of Saul, and Nathan was a court prophet for King David. Elijah and his successor, Elisha, are important prophets in the northern kingdom of Israel. Elijah insisted on the exclusive worship of Yahweh; according to the Deuteronomistic Historians, worship of false gods was a major sin in the northern kingdom. Elijah has particular uniqueness in that he is only one of two people who go to heaven without dying (the other is Enoch in Genesis).

"Neviim" refers to the books of the prophets in the Hebrew Scriptures. It has two divisions: the Former Prophets (which consist of the books of Joshua, Judges, Samuel, and Kings) and the Latter Prophets which can be further divided into the Major Prophets (so named because of the length of the books and not because they are more important) and the Minor Prophets. These "minor prophets" are known as The Twelve. Several of these prophets lived and prophesized during the period of the divided kingdoms. **Amos** preached to the people of the northern kingdom of Israel (although he was a native of Judea) during the reign of King Jeroboam II (786–746). His message was that because of Israel's social injustice and not following God, they would be militarily conquered. **Hosea** was prophesying in Israel in about that same time period. God told Hosea to marry a woman named Gomer, who would be unfaithful. Hosea uses his own marriage as a metaphor for Israel's relationship to God. Hosea's writings alternate between discussions of his marriage and Israel's unfaithfulness to God. Hosea is forgiving to his wife, and God continues to love Israel although Israel must repent and change its ways.

Micah was a prophet in Judea during the reigns of Jotham (742–735), Ahaz (735–715), and Hezekiah (715–687). Micah preached against the religious and political leaders of that time for the lack of social justice. Instead of looking out for the common good, they were more interested in personal self-interests.

Isaiah is actually believed to be the composite of several different prophets. "First Isaiah" prophesized in Jerusalem during the reigns of kings Uzziah, Jotham, Ahaz, and Hezekiah (738 to 701–688) and was a contemporary of Micah. Chapters 1–39 for the most part are attributed to "First Isaiah." Chapters 40–55 are attributed to "Second Isaiah" or "Deutero-Isaiah." Chapters 56–66 are attributed to

"Trito-Isaiah." Chapters 40–55 cover a time period during the Babylonian exile (597–539). Chapters 56–66 cover a time period between 520 and 515, when people have returned from exile to Judah. The messages of "First Isaiah" included predictions of divine punishment for social inequalities and injustices. "First Isaiah" said that religious ritual was not of prime importance, and the importance of social justice was stressed.

> Wash yourselves; make yourselves clean;
> remove the evil of your doings from before my eyes;
> cease to do evil, learn to do good;
> seek justice, rescue the oppressed, defend the
> orphan, plead for the widow. (Isa. 1:16–17)

Nahum was a prophet during the reign of King Josiah (640–609). Nahum prophesized that Nineveh, the capital of Assyria, would be punished for its domination of many small countries, including Judah, and the destruction of the northern kingdom of Israel. The Lord will deliver Judah.

Zephaniah was also prophesying during this time period. He may have been a disciple of Isaiah. The message of Zephaniah was that "the day of the Lord approaches" in which there will be judgment on Judah and on Judah's enemies due to worship of false gods and social injustices.

Habakkuk likely was a prophet during the reign of King Jehoiakim (609–598). He complains to God about the violence and the evil in the world, and although not explicitly named, the Babylonians are the perceived culprits. The book ends with a hymn describing Yahweh as the divine warrior against the cosmic forces of evil.

Jeremiah had a long career, spanning from the 13th year of King Josiah (627) until the fall of Jerusalem in 586. Jeremiah warned Judeans to learn from the mistakes of the northern kingdom of Israel:

> For if you truly amend your ways and your doings, if you truly act justly one with another, if you do not oppress the alien, the orphan, and the widow, or shed innocent blood in this place, and if you do not go after other gods to your own hurt, then I will dwell with you in this place, in the land that I gave of old to your ancestors forever and ever. (Jer. 7:5–7)

The Judeans do not heed this, and God sends King Nebuchadnezzar of Babylon—"my servant" —to lay waste to the land of Judah. Many Judeans are made captive and are sent to Babylon in exile. Jeremiah, writing from Judah, sends a message to those in Babylon:

> Thus says the Lord of hosts, the God of Israel, to all the exiles whom I have sent into exile from Jerusalem to Babylon: Build houses and live in them; plant gardens and eat what they produce. Take wives and have sons and daughters; take wives for your sons, and give your daughters in marriage, that they may bear sons and daughters; multiply there, and do not decrease. But seek the peace of the city to which I have exiled you, and pray to the Lord on its behalf, for in its welfare you will find your welfare. (Jer. 29:4–7)

What was stressed by these prophets was the need to stay faithful to Yahweh, social justice, and the need to take care of those who are less fortunate.

The Babylonian Period
(600 to 540 B.C.E.)

In 605 B.C.E. the joint armies of Assyria and Egypt were defeated by the Babylonians. King Jehoiakim was a loyal vassal of Egypt, and now with this defeat of the Egyptian army he became a vassal of Babylon. After some time he rebelled against the king of Babylon by refusing to pay tribute, and King Nebuchadnezzar of Babylon prepared to attack Judah in response. During this period Jehoiakim died, and his son Jehoiachin became king. Nebuchadnezzar reasserted control. There were three waves of deportations of Judeans to Babylon.

- The first exile took place in 597 B.C.E. The Babylonians ransacked the temple and stole treasures from the kingdom, but they did not destroy the city of Jerusalem. King Jehoiachin, along with several thousand of the most important citizens of Jerusalem, were brought to Babylon in exile. The prophet Ezekiel was one of the citizens brought to Babylon. Nebuchadnezzar appointed Zedekiah as king of Judah.
- Jerusalem was again attacked in 587 B.C.E. Zedekiah had asserted independence from Babylon, and Babylon retaliated. Zedekiah was taken prisoner and brought to Babylon along with more of the elite citizens of Judah. Solomon's temple was destroyed.
- In 582 B.C.E. there were more deportations of Judeans by the Babylonians (Jer. 52:30) in response to some revolts in Judea.

Although many Judeans were sent into exile in Babylon, many other Judeans remained in Judea. Thus there were two separate groups of Judeans. Those in Babylon (the Diaspora —those who had been dispersed) lived in communities with other Judeans and were permitted to live according to their own customs. The exiles had no temples for worship, and so new forms of worship developed. This was the beginning of the synagogue. No longer were sacrifices made. Both prophets Jeremiah and Ezekiel felt that Yahweh was with the exiles rather than those who were left behind. Jeremiah referred to the exiles as "good figs" and those who remained in the land as "bad figs."

The exile was an important time period for the coming together of the Torah. Two extremely important works were products of this time period: The Priestly Source (P) and a revision of the Deuteronomistic History and the book of **Deuteronomy**. Temple priests were exiled to Babylon. They had no temple to attend to there, but they continued to have importance. It has been suggested to think of there being a "priestly school" analogous to the Deuteronomists. Ezekiel was considered to be part of this school. "P" was an important source in the books of **Genesis, Exodus, Leviticus,** and **Numbers**. They addressed how to preserve their religious identity in a foreign land and without the temple. They stressed adherence to dietary laws, keeping the Sabbath, and observing circumcision.

It was during this time period that at least the core of the Torah came together, i.e., the combining of "J," "E," "D," "P," and "H" (the Holiness Code in chapters 17–26 of Leviticus). After returning from exile to Judah, the prophet Ezra produces "the book of the law of Moses" (Neh. 8:1). This is the first mention of there being a book for the followers of Yahweh.

Lamentations is a collection of reactions to the destruction of Jerusalem in 586. It was written by one or more poets who grieve for Jerusalem although it's felt that the destruction was deserved punishment.

Obadiah is the shortest book of the Hebrew Bible (21 verses) and is devoted to divine judgment of Edom (the people said to be descendants of Esau, the brother of Jacob). Edomites assisted the Babylonians in the destruction of Jerusalem in 586. This is also the subject of Psalm 137 (the psalms come from many different periods in the Israelites' history).

There was debate about whether the book of **Ezekiel** should be part of the canon of Scripture. Ezekiel was deported by Nebuchadnezzar to Babylon in the first deportation in 597. He was a contemporary of Jeremiah. Ezekiel was an unusual character, prone to some bizarre behaviors. There have been suggestions that he may have had a seizure disorder or was schizophrenic. Ezekiel believed the Babylonian exile and the destruction of Jerusalem were deserved punishments for idolatry, ritual impurity, and violence.

When one nation conquered another nation in those days, it was common to attribute the victory to the conquering nation's superior gods. The Judeans did not do this. Instead they blamed their defeats and woes to their own sinfulness. There was no conception in those days for a theology of "bad things happen to good people."

One very important voice during this time period was Deutero-Isaiah, or **Second Isaiah** (his writings are chapters 40–55 of the book of Isaiah). He saw the return from Babylon to Judea as a new exodus. He is the first voice to clearly and unambiguously state that Yahweh is the only God, not just the god of the Israelites.

> I am the first and I am the last; besides me there is no god. (Isa. 44:6)

Wisdom literature was another popular genre in the ancient Near East; it is concerned with various realities of the universal human experience. The book of **Job** in the Bible is one example. We will see two other examples in the Persian period: Ecclesiastes and Proverbs. Both Job and Ecclesiastes are interesting in that they address issues of "theodicy," and they take an unorthodox view for their time. Theodicy has to do with why pain and suffering occur in the world. In polytheistic societies this was explained by there being good and bad gods. One would make sacrifices to gods to try to gain their favor. With monotheism (the existence of only one God) where God is responsible for everything that happens, what is the explanation for calamity? The orthodox explanation would be that righteousness is rewarded and evilness is punished. The books of Job and Ecclesiastes take different views, and these views are also found in other literature of the ancient Near East.

The book of Job begins with "There was once a man in the land of Uz whose name was Job. That man was blameless and upright, one who feared God and turned away from evil" (Job 1:1). Satan, one of God's council in heaven, pointed out to God that Job's life was wonderful and questioned whether he would still be faithful if his life was not so wonderful. So God allowed Satan to cause adversity for Job. His seven sons and three daughters were killed as were his servants and livestock. Job remained faithful to God. Then Job was afflicted with "loathsome sores" "from the sole of his foot to the crown of his head." Job remained faithful to God. . . for a while. He later curses the day he was born: "Why did I not die at birth, come forth from the womb and expire?" (Job 3:11). Job's friends tell him that his troubles must be the result of some sin he's committed, consistent with the prevailing beliefs of that time of retributive justice. However, we know that this is not the case; the narrator at the beginning of the book of Job already has told us that that he was "blameless and upright." Most of the book of Job consists of his complaining to God about his woes. At the end of the book Job's fortunes are reversed, and he ends up having twice as much as he did before.

The book of Job is difficult to date, but the prevailing thought would be sometime in the exilic period. If so, a related theodicy issue is an explanation for the destruction of God's temple. The prevailing explanation at that time period for such events would be that the Babylonian god, Marduk, must be superior to Yaweh. There were many similar texts similar to the story of Job during this time period, including Babylonian, Sumerian, and Egyptian writings.

The Persian Period
(540 to 330 B.C.E.)

In 539, Cyrus, the king of Persia, defeated the Babylonians. The Persians were the great power in the area at the time. This marks the beginning of the "Persian Period," otherwise known in regards to Judah as the "postexilic period." Cyrus decreed that the Judeans (and other exiled peoples) could return to their homelands. He encouraged a resumption of their customs, religions, and rituals. He encouraged the Judeans to rebuild the temple in Jerusalem, and he even returned riches stolen from the temple by Nebuchadnezzar. Judeans viewed Cyrus as "God's anointed."

Most of the exiles did not return to Judea. They had homes, families, new lives. The relatively small group who did return to Judea built an altar when they arrived in Jerusalem so that they could resume making sacrifices to Yahweh. A year later they started construction on a new temple. It was dedicated in 515, and at that time rituals resumed there (in accordance with directions in the Torah).

Haggai and **Zechariah** were two prophets during this time period, and they supported and encouraged the building of the temple. Haggai hoped for the reestablishment of the Davidic monarchy. The message of Zechariah's visions was the destruction of Babylon, the restoration of Jerusalem and the temple, and establishing divinely chosen leaders to rule the community. According to Zechariah, people from all over the world would come to Jerusalem's temple to worship Yahweh.

"Trito-Isaiah," or **"Third Isaiah,"** is the writer of chapters 56–66 of the book of that name. He is writing during the time that the temple has been restored and is functioning. Third Isaiah speaks of a more inclusive community now in Judea where foreigners will be included. He, like many of his prophetic predecessors, emphasizes the importance of social justice over ritual observances.

Ezra and **Nehemiah** are two separate books in the Christian Bible, but, in all likelihood, they were originally a single work and remain a single work in the Hebrew Bible. The books get their names from the two principal characters, Ezra and Nehemiah. The book(s) were compiled from a variety of sources (part of Ezra was written in Aramaic rather than Hebrew). Ezra was "a scribe skilled in the Torah of Moses," and he is mentioned in Nehemiah as reading the Torah during a festival. Ezra stressed the importance of keeping all the commandments of the Lord and in particular stressed that the Hebrews should not intermarry, should observe the Sabbath, and should support the temple by paying an annual tax. Nehemiah was a governor of Judah who led the project to rebuild the walls around Jerusalem.

The postexilic period saw the emergence of a new genre known as "apocalyptic" literature. A "genre" is a category of literature, such as romance novels or science fiction. Apocalyptic literature appeared to have developed out of prophecy; vision and dreams are common to both. Common elements of apocalyptic literature include divine revelations, pessimism about the present but optimism about the future, a dualistic perspective (i.e., good vs. evil), and descriptions of end times. A few early forms of apocalyptic literature appeared during this time: the **"Isaiah Apocalypse"** (chapters 24–27), **"Second Zechariah"** (like Isaiah, it was felt that Zechariah was written by two and possibly three writers), **Joel**, and **Malachi**.

First and Second Chronicles were originally a single book. It covers a period all the way back to Adam and up to the return of exiles to Judea, although it's main focus is on the events covered in 1-2 Kings and 1-2 Samuel. It was written in the late Persian period, and it is a revisionist history in which the Davidic kings were idealized (for example, in regards to King David none of the unpleasant events were reported such as the affair with Bathsheba and the arrangement of her husband's death). The sources for the chronicler included the Deuteronomistic History, the

Pentateuch, Psalms, Isaiah, Jeremiah, Ezekiel, Ezra, and sources that are no longer available to us (e.g., prophecy of Ahijah the Shilonite, visions of the seer Iddo, etc.).

The book of **Psalms** is an anthology of hymns that probably was edited into its final form in the late fourth century B.C.E. It is the result of a long process of compilation and editing. Some hymns are attributed to King David (although probably significantly less was actually written by him than have been attributed to him by various sources). These types of hymns and poems were commonplace throughout the ancient Near East.

The book of **Proverbs** is in the genre of "wisdom literature" that we discussed previously. It contains pithy words of wisdom. This anthology also was likely compiled in the late fourth century B.C.E. Some examples from Proverbs include:

> A capable wife who can find? She is far more precious than jewels. (Prov. 31:10)
> Speak out, judge righteously, defend the rights of the poor and needy. (Prov. 31:9)
> Whoever loves discipline loves knowledge, but those who hate to be rebuked are stupid. (Prov. 12:1)
> A soft answer turns away wrath, but a harsh word stirs up anger. (Prov. 15:1)

The book of **Ecclesiastes** contains very unorthodox views, and thus there was controversy as to whether it should have been included in the Bible. It was attributed (falsely) to Solomon at one time, which was why it was probably included. There is some controversy as to whether it was written in the Persian or the Greek period. It is a collection of musings about the meaning of life. The author states that goodness is not always rewarded, and sin is not always punished. No matter if you're righteous or evil, we all die. It is recommended then to enjoy life while it is there. The famous phrase "eat, drink, and be merry" comes from this book.

The **Song of Solomon** also comes from this time period. This is also an unusual piece of biblical literature. It is an anthology of erotic love poems. Again, because it was attributed at one time to Solomon (falsely), it was included in the canon. Later commentators interpreted the work allegorically, i.e., love poems to the church. Others draw other meanings from the work, such as the transforming power of love between a man and woman in marriage. Others see it as a book of secular love poems celebrating erotic love.

The book of **Jonah** was probably written in the postexilic period and is a fictional narrative. The setting of the story is the Assyrian period. Jonah is a prophet called by God to preach to the city of Nineveh, the capital of Assyria, the enemy of Israel and Judah. Jonah does not want to do this and boards a ship headed in the opposite direction. Yahweh sends a storm, and the ship is close to sinking. Very interestingly, the non-Israelite sailors are presented as more pious than the prophet, Jonah. They pray to their gods for help, and even after learning that the cause of the storm is Jonah, they refuse to throw him off the ship until they have no choice. It is here that the famous story occurs of Jonah being swallowed by a giant fish (not a whale). Jonah prays in the fish's stomach, and after three days is vomited up. Jonah then heads to Nineveh and when there preaches for the inhabitants to repent. The people, including the king, do repent, and Nineveh is saved. This infuriates Jonah who wanted to see the city destroyed. The lesson is that Yahweh cares for all people, even the livestock of the Assyrians.

Like the book of Jonah, the book of **Esther** is another fictional narrative set in the past. This time the setting is the early Persian Period. It was probably written a century later. Interestingly, it is a secular book in which God is not even mentioned. Esther is a Jewish exile who becomes wife and queen to the Persian king. Esther basically won a beauty contest in order to be the new queen. The king's right hand man, Haman, plots against his enemy, Mordecai (Esther's Jewish cousin) and all the Jewish people by telling the king that the Jews refuse to obey his laws (the king does not know that his wife, Esther, is Jewish). Esther intervenes and saves the Jewish people.

The Greek Period
(330 to 170 B.C.E.)

The Persians and the Greeks were the two great powers in that part of the world. Around 330 B.C.E. the Greeks prevailed under the leadership of Alexander the Great and controlled the entire Near East. Not only did they politically control the area, but they also culturally changed it. This was known as Hellenization; Greek culture, language, and ideas transformed many peoples, including the Jewish people. Greek became the dominant language in the area; the entire New Testament was written in Greek.

At the age of only 33, Alexander died. The Greek Empire then was divided into three parts. The Ptolemaic Empire was in Egypt and was then ruled by a succession of rulers who took the name "Ptolemy" rather than "pharaoh." Rule passed from father to son. The Ptolemaic capital city was Alexandria. The Seleucid Empire was in Asia and included Persia. Its capital was Antioch. Greece itself was ruled by the Antigonid dynasty.

The land of Judea was between the Ptolemaic Empire in the South and the Seleucid Empire in the North. During most of the third century B.C.E. Judea was under the control of the Ptolemies, and under this rule they had a lot of independence in regards to worship. There were a number of wars between the Ptolemaics and the Seleucids and with the Fifth Syrian War at the end of the third century, the Egyptians were defeated, and Judea went under Syrian Seleucid control.

The book of **Daniel** is the only book of the Hebrew canon that was written in this period and is the latest work to be included in the Hebrew canon. Its author (or authors) is unknown. It is the fictitious account of a Jewish hero, Daniel, who was a Jewish exile in Babylon during the sixth century B.C.E. Much of the material of chapters 1–6 (which are stories about the character, Daniel) likely originated in the fourth and third centuries. Scholars believe that the book took its final form sometime around 167 B.C.E. Some of the book is written in Hebrew and some in Aramaic.

Chapters 7–12 of the book of **Daniel** contain four visions of the character, Daniel. These chapters are examples of the genre of literature called "apocalyptic." In addition to the examples we talked about previously which were somewhat apocalyptic (chapters 24–27 of Isaiah, Second Zechariah, Joel and Malachi), other examples are the books of 1 Enoch, 4 Ezra, 2 Baruch, and, in the New Testament, the book of Revelation. The first half of the book of **Daniel** shows the example of a man who remains faithful to Jewish law while serving a foreign ruler (Nebuchadnezzar). The second half describes end times when the dead will be resurrected and God will prevail over the forces of evil.

There were some additions to the book of Daniel that are not in the Hebrew Scriptures, but are in the Greek version of the Scriptures, the Septuagint, and also were included in the Catholic and Eastern Orthodox canon of the Hebrew Scriptures. These additions are The Prayer of Azariah, The Song of the Three Jews, the stories of Susanna, and Bel and the Dragon.

Tobit probably dates to the early Hellenistic Period. It is not part of the Hebrew canon. The setting of the story is the Diaspora among those who were exiled by the Assyrians from the northern kingdom of Israel. Tobit is a pious Jew living in Nineveh, the capital of Assyria. A number of events happen in this story including droppings from a sparrow falling into Tobit's eye and blinding him, being attacked by a giant fish which Tobit kills, using the heart and liver of the fish to fend off demons, using the gall of the fish to cure his blindness, and being accompanied on the journey by a relative who in reality is an angel. After all the events, Tobit offers a prayer to God in which there is a suggestion that the dispersion of the Israelites was not just due to sinful behavior, but also as a means of spreading the knowledge about God to the rest of the world. The book also offers instructions on how to be faithful to God when there is no temple to make sacrifices. Tobit emphasizes ethical behaviors (giving food and clothing to the poor and loving others), eating kosher food, and not intermarrying.

Chapter 3

The Intertestamental Period

Timeline of Important Events

167	Maccabean revolt
165	Rededication of the temple
190–180	Ben Sira writes book of Wisdom
167	Hasmonean uprising
164	Judah Maccabee retakes Jerusalem; temple reconsecrated
160–142	Jonathan leads Hasmonean uprising; Jewish sects first appear in Judea
141–63	Hasmoneans rule independent Jewish state and kingdom
63	Roman army captures Judea

The Maccabean Period
(170 to 63 B.C.E.)

Although still a part of the Hellenistic or Greek Period which continues until the Roman conquest in 70 B.C.E., a new period for the Jews occurs in 164. The Seleucids rather than the Ptolemaics were governing the Hebrew people. A revolt by the Jewish people took place due to Jews being prohibited from practicing their religion. A Greek gymnasium and stadium were built in Jerusalem, and a statue to a foreign deity (Baal?) was installed in the temple. This pushed the Jewish people over the edge, and they revolted. They gained control over Jerusalem, and in 164 they purified and rededicated the temple. This event is still commemorated today as Hanukkah. This began a period of self-rule once again known as the "Hasmonean" rule. From 110 to 63 B.C.E. Israel was an independent kingdom again.

There were a number of important writings during this time period. **First Maccabees** gives an account of the Judean revolt against Antiochus IV and the Seleucids and covers the time period from 185 to 135 B.C.E. Because it was written in Greek, it was not included in the Jewish canon. However, it is an important piece of historical literature, especially as it gives an account of the origin of Hanukkah. Interestingly, though, God is not explicitly mentioned in the work.

Second Maccabees is another account of the Maccabean revolt but covering a shorter period of time (175 to 161 B.C.E.). This too was written in Greek. It is more religious than 1 Maccabees and reiterates the old theme of God rewarding the good and punishing the wicked. This writing also was not included in the Hebrew canon. One interesting topic that is mentioned in this book (as well as the book of Daniel) is the concept of the resurrection of the dead. These are among the first instances in which this concept is first clearly articulated. It was believed to be granted only to the righteous, and it appears that the author of 2 Maccabees believed that prayer and sacrifice could help in gaining eternal reward for the deceased.

The book of **Baruch** was probably originally written in Hebrew. It was purportedly written by Baruch, the scribe of the prophet Jeremiah, although it likely was actually written much later in the second century B.C.E. The book appears to be a composite of three separate texts. It was not included in the Jewish canon.

The **Wisdom of Ben Sira or Sirach** is a book named after its actual author. Although not included in the Jewish canon, it was a writing widely used by Jews in the Diaspora. It is a collection of wisdom sayings, much like the book of Proverbs. Ben Sira lived in Jerusalem during the late third and early second centuries and was a scholar of the Jewish Scriptures.

The **Wisdom of Solomon** was originally written in Greek and so not included in the Jewish canon. Although tradition attributed it to Solomon, its being written in Greek and containing many Greek philosophical concepts, it was obviously not written by Solomon. It is believed by scholars to have been written in Alexandria, Egypt, somewhere between the first century B.C.E. and the first century C.E. It is one of the earliest Jewish writings to present a doctrine of the immortality of the soul. Although the early Hebrew Scriptures describe a place called Sheol (much the same as Hades in early Greek mythology), it is a miserable and shadowy place where all people go after death, regardless if they have been righteous or evil. The book of Ecclesiastes says: "The living know that they will die, but the dead know nothing; they have no more reward, and even the memory of them is lost. Their love and their hate and their envy have already perished; never again will they have any share in all that happens under the sun" (Eccles. 9:5–6), "for there is no work or thought or knowledge or wisdom in Sheol, to which you are going" (Eccles. 9:10). It is in The Wisdom of Solomon that we are presented with the idea that individuals have a soul (the word "psyche," the Greek word for soul, is used a couple dozen times in the book), and that there are two different fates for the righteous and the evil. The wicked go to Hades. "But the righteous live forever, and their reward is with the Lord; the Most High takes care of them. Therefore they will receive a glorious crown and a beautiful diadem from the hand of the Lord, because with his right hand he will cover them, and with his arm he will shield them" (Wis 5:15–16). This book speaks of the immortality of the soul only, not the physical resurrection of the dead as in the book of Daniel. How does one achieve this immortality? The answer is by the pursuit of wisdom. The Wisdom of Solomon addresses the theodicy quandary, i.e., why do good things happen to the wicked and bad things to the righteous? The answer is that all get their just desserts in the end, although perhaps not in this life.

The book of **Judith**, like the book of Esther, is about a fictional character. It was likely written after the Maccabean revolt. Although probably translated to Greek from Hebrew or Aramaic, it is not included in the Jewish canon. The setting of the story is Judea, but the time period of the story is confusing due to many historical inaccuracies. In the story, Nebuchadnezzar is reported as the king of the Assyrians (he actually was a Babylonian king). Nebuchadnezzar sent his general, Holofernes to lead the Assyrian army in an attack against the Israelites. Before this can happen he meets Judith and is captivated by her beauty. They have dinner; Holfernes plans to have sex with Judith but becomes drunk and passes out. Judith cuts off his head, which is placed on the wall of the city. The Assyrian army sees this, and because of their shock and panic they are able to be defeated by the Israelites.

Third Maccabees was likely written in the first century B.C.E., and it was written in Greek. It has a misleading title in that it has nothing to do with the Maccabean uprising. It is a historical fiction set a century earlier during the reign of Ptolemy IV Philopator (201–204). Ptolemy wished to visit the temple in Jerusalem, and he was told he could not enter the "holy of holies." When he insisted that he go in there, the high priest prayed for divine intervention, and Ptolemy had a stroke. He returned to Egypt. He decreed that the Jews must give up their worship of Yahweh and instead worship the Greek god Dionysus. Most Jews in Egypt refused, and so Ptolemy rounded them up and placed them in the Hippodrome, a stadium, along with 500 intoxicated elephants. Because of intervention by God's angels, the elephants did not attack the Jews but rather Ptolemy's men. Ptolemy repented. The Jews then executed the Jews who had turned from their faith.

Fourth Maccabees also is not part of the Jewish canon. It was composed in Greek, and its likely date of composition is between the first and the second century C.E. It also is notable for its belief in the immortality of the soul and the belief in divine rewards and retributions. The book also stresses the importance of reason over emotions and the importance of being faithful to Mosaic law.

63

The book of 1 **Enoch** is not part of the Jewish canon and neither is it part of the Apocrypha, although it is of some importance. It is mentioned in the book of Jude in the New Testament. It was attributed to the prophet Enoch, who is mentioned in the book of Genesis in chapter 5:21–24. Enoch and the prophet Elijah are the only two people in the Bible to be taken directly to God without dying. First Enoch discusses the origins of evil (fallen angels, Satan) and a day of judgment in which the righteous will be granted peace and the wicked will be destroyed. The books of 1 Enoch and Daniel are the first books in Hebrew tradition to describe in detail judgment after death and an ultimate resurrection.

Hebrew Canon

"Canon" is the term for scriptural writings that are considered authoritative and standard for determining "orthodox" beliefs. The five books of the Torah were the first to be given canonical status, and this may have happened as early as the fifth century B.C.E.

The Hebrew Scriptures consist of three groups of writings: The Torah (Genesis, Exodus, Leviticus, Numbers, and Deuteronomy), the Prophets (which includes the two divisions of the Former Prophets and the Latter Prophets), and the Writings (which is a variety of writings from different genres).

The Torah (Hebrew for "teaching"), also known as the Pentateuch (from a Greek word meaning "Five Scrolls"), have traditionally been ascribed to the prophet and lawgiver Moses. Scholars, however, are almost unanimous in their conclusions that these books were not written by Moses.

First of all, Moses never identifies himself as the author. In Deuteronomy, Moses's death and burial were described making it unlikely that Moses was the writer. The books were not written in first-person narrative, also suggesting that someone else was the author (e.g.it is written "Then Moses answered" rather than "Then I answered"). There are historical details in the books that would have happened much later in history. For example, the Philistines are mentioned, and they would not have arrived in Palestine until at least a century after the time of Moses. In Gen. 36:31 it says "These are the kings who reigned in the land of Edom, before any king reigned over the Israelites." This suggests that the author is aware that there would be kings who would reign in a nation called Israel.

Also in reading these books it becomes apparent that different passages are pieced together from different sources making the narrative quite redundant at times. One example of two different narratives being pieced together is the story of the creation. There are two different creation stories in Genesis. The first is in chapter 1, and the second is in chapters 2–3. They are quite different from each other.

Genesis 1	**Genesis 2–3**
In the beginning was watery chaos	World is a rainless landscape
Animals are created before humans	First human is made, then animals
Humans are created male and female	Woman is formed from man's rib
No mention of Garden of Eden	No mention of seven days
No mention of tree of life	No mention of heavenly bodies
No mention of tree of knowledge	No mention of divine rest
No mention of disobedience	
No mention of divine punishment	

The second group of writing in the Old Testament is "The Prophets." These are further divided into two groups: the former prophets and the latter prophets. The former prophets include the books of Joshua, Judges, Samuel, and Kings. This is sometimes called the "Deuteronomistic History." It gives the history of the Israelites from the time of Joshua, through the time of the judges, through the united kingdom, through the divided kingdoms, and up until the Babylonian exile. The history is referred to as "Deuteronomistic" because throughout this history the narrative examines how well the Israelite people follow the law outlined in Deuteronomy.

The latter prophets can be divided into two groups: the Major Prophets (the longer books of Isaiah, Jeremiah, and Ezekiel) and the Minor Prophets (Hosea, Joel, Amos, Obadiah, Jonah, Micah, Nahum, Habakkuk, Zephaniah, Haggai, Zechariah, and Malachi), sometimes referred to as "The Twelve."

The third division of the Jewish canon is "The Writings." This includes the books of Chronicles which covers the same historical period as that covered in the books of Samuel and Kings, but from a different perspective. It includes also the books of Ezra and Nehemiah which extends the narrative account to the restoration of the Israelite people as a subject people under the Persian Empire. These four books have been said to have been written by the "Chronicler," although it is not certain whether it was the same author for each of these four books. The Writings also include what scholars characterize as "historical fiction" in the books of Ruth, Esther, and Daniel. It also includes the poetical books of Psalms, Proverbs, Song of Solomon, and Lamentations. Also included is the book of Job and the book of Ecclesiastes.

So the Hebrew Bible as we know it did not take final shape until the second century C.E. There is some controversy by scholars whether a formal council (there was a gathering of rabbis at the Palestinian coastal town of Jabneh around 90 C.E.) was responsible for deciding which books were canonical, or whether the canon developed in more of an informal way. Some criteria for being included in the canon included being written before the fourth century B.C.E., being written in Hebrew, and being extensively used.

There is the belief that certain writings have been "inspired" by God. This does not mean that the words came verbatim by God; the only writings that are claimed to be the verbatim words of God are those of the Qur'an. Muhammad claimed that he was transcribing the actual words of God. Being "inspired" and being "canonical" are not synonymous. "Inspiration" is the broader term. Many writings were considered as being "inspired" by God but were not included in any canon.

The Septuagint

The Septuagint is the Greek translation of the Hebrew Scriptures. You might recall that after the Babylonian exile Jews were dispersed throughout the Near East. Greek became the language that was *lingua franca*, the common language that was used throughout the region. The Torah was translated first in the third century B.C.E. Legend has it that 72 Jewish scholars (six from each of the 12 tribes of Israel) were each put into 72 separate chambers with the task of translating the Torah from Hebrew to Greek. Remarkably, according to the legend, each translation was exactly the same. Over the next two to three centuries the rest of the Hebrew Scriptures were translated into Greek. The Septuagint contains additional writings that the Hebrew Bible does not have. These have come to be known as Apocrypha. It was the Septuagint that was primarily read during the time of Jesus.

The Apocrypha

The term "Apocrypha" literally means "hidden." These books also are designated as "deuterocanonical," meaning that they belong to a second canon. They are not part of the Hebrew canon, but they are part of the Septuagint, and they are part of the Christian Bible (both Roman Catholic and Orthodox), although at the time of the Reformation they were removed from the Bible by the Protestant reformers. These are the books that are in the Roman Catholic canon and in the Eastern Orthodox canon:

Roman Catholic	**Eastern Orthodox**
	1 Esdras
	2 Esdras
Tobit	Tobit
Judith	Judith
1 Maccabees	1 Maccabees
2 Maccabees	2 Maccabees
	3 Maccabees
Wisdom of Solomon	Wisdom of Solomon
Sirach	Sirach
Baruch	Baruch
	Letter of Jeremiah
	(4 Maccabees)

Chapter 4

Writing the New Testament

Timeline of Important Events

63 B.C.E.	Roman army captures Judea
37–4	Kingdom of Herod the Great
4 B.C.E.?	Birth of Jesus
6 C.E.	Judea becomes Roman province; first appearance of the "Fourth Philosophy"
30 C.E.	Jesus' death
33 C.E.	Conversion of Paul
50–60 C.E.	Pauline Epistles
50–60	Q Source
50–70	M and L Sources
65	Gospel of Mark
66–70 C.E.	Jewish uprising against Rome
70 C.E.	Fall of Jerusalem; Second Temple is destroyed
80–85?	Gospels of Matthew and Luke, Book of Acts
80–100	Deutero-Pauline Epistles, 1 Peter, Hebrews, James
85–105?	Pastoral Epistles
90–95?	Gospel of John
95?	Book of Revelation
120?	2 Peter
110–130?	Gospels of Peter and Thomas
132–135	Bar Kokhba Uprising
285–337	Constantine

The Early Roman Period
(63 B.C.E. to 100 C.E.)

The Middle East was dominated by a succession of empires: the Assyrians, then the Babylonians, then the Persians, then the Greeks, and now the Romans. After defeating their primary rival in the western Mediterranean, the Carthaginians, at the end of the third century B.C.E., they began expanding east. In 63 B.C.E. Palestine was conquered by the Roman general Pompey. Herod "the Great" was made king of the Jews and reigned from 40 to 4 B.C.E. Herod was made king by Roman decree and was not of the Davidic line. He also had no links to the monarchy of the Hasmoneans. During this time, Octavian, who was Julius Caesar's adopted son, became emperor. He became known as Caesar Augustus. While Rome's influence had been expanding since the sixth century B.C.E., the Roman Empire as we understand it began with Caesar Augustus.

The Historical Jesus

Jesus was born in 4 B.C.E. and lived until 30 C.E. Scholars are convinced that the man, Jesus, existed and was crucified by the Romans. Despite the tremendous influence he has had on the world, little was written about him during the actual time period of his life. His life had little impact on society during the time he was living. Nothing was written about him in pagan sources during that time, and there were very few references to him in Jewish sources. One exception is the Jewish historian Josephus who talks about Jesus in *The Antiquities of the Jews*. Primarily what has been written about him has come almost exclusively by his followers who were in fact not eyewitnesses to the events. The books about

Jesus were written decades after his life and in Greek, not the language of Jesus and his followers which was Aramaic. Stories about Jesus were transmitted orally until they were finally written down decades later.

Judaism changed a great deal after the completion of the books in the Hebrew Bible. Far more Jews were living outside of Judea in the Diaspora than in Judea. Large communities of Jews were in Babylonia (territories of modern day Iraq and Iran), Egypt (particularly Alexandria), Asia Minor (modern day Turkey), areas of modern day Syria and Lebanon, and smaller communities in Greece, Macedonia, Crete, Cyprus, Rome, and some areas of Spain. With less access to the temple in Jerusalem, Jews had to find new ways to worship God. Prayer and reading of the Torah grew in importance, and sacrifices at the temple became less central in the religion. Synagogues provided alternatives to the temple in Jerusalem for worship. It was in the synagogues that Jews were educated about what it means to be Jewish. Hebrew Scripture was read aloud, and this was followed by instruction by priests or elders about the meaning of the words (i.e., some type of sermon). Prayer appears to have been part of synagogue activity, although it was not mentioned in Judea prior to the destruction of the temple in 70 C.E. (sacrifice was what was important—not prayer).

There was much diversity of thought amongst Jews during the time of Jesus. It is important to recognize that Judaism was non-creedal; there were no "orthodox" beliefs that one had to subscribe to. What was important was following the law, not in believing a certain way. Some of this diversity is reflected in the four major sects (or schools of thought) at that time: The Pharisees, Sadducees, Essenes, and the

"Fourth Philosophy." These various sects first emerged during the rule of the Hasmoneans. Most Jews did not belong to any of these groups.

The Pharisees represented the largest of these groups (perhaps 6,000 members). They were very intent upon keeping the law of Moses as strictly as possible. Since some of these laws are ambiguous (for example, how does one "keep the Sabbath day holy"?), they devised specific rules and regulations for keeping the law. These rules and regulations came to be known as the "oral law." This oral tradition eventually was written down around 200 C.E. and now is known as the "Mishnah." Pharisees believed in the resurrection of the dead and an afterlife (although it is not certain whether this included the physical bodies or just the soul). Evil souls were eternally imprisoned, and good souls get a new life.

The Sadducees were a much smaller group than the Pharisees but were much more powerful. They were members of the Jewish aristocracy. It appears that they considered only the Torah (the five books of Moses) as being authoritative. They were less focused on keeping the letter of the law and were more concerned about the temple and sacrificial worship. They denied the notion of a resurrection of the soul or the existence of angels. They may have believed that the soul dies with the body at the time of death. It is also possible that they believed in the existence of Sheol, a shadowy existence for all of the dead (no matter how one lived their life).

The Essenes were the second largest sect (perhaps 4,000 members). Although this group was not mentioned in New Testament writings, they are the group responsible for the writings we found in the famous "Dead Sea Scrolls." These scrolls were discovered in a cave by accident in 1947 by a shepherd boy in Qumran, near the western shore of the Dead Sea. There were at least partial copies of every book in the Hebrew Scriptures, with the exception of the book of Esther. What makes this find remarkable and valuable is that these writings were nearly a *thousand* years older than any biblical writings we had previously possessed. The Essenes expected an imminent end of times, an apocalypse in which there would be a final battle between the forces of good and evil. God would triumph, and there would be a new kingdom on earth ruled by two messiahs: a king of the lineage of David and a priest. Like the Pharisees, the Essenes believed in the immortality of the soul. Although predating early Christians, scholars have seen some similarities between the two groups, including communal living and baptism. The Essenes withdrew from mainstream Jewish society and lived in monastic communes (only males) and maintained celibacy.

The last of these four sects was known as the Fourth Philosophy, and they were intent on overthrowing Roman rule. The Zealots were a subgroup of this philosophy. Around 6 C.E., during the time of Jesus' childhood, a revolutionary named Judas the Galilean led a revolt against the Romans because of a census which was imposed for tax purposes. The uprising was immediately crushed. The revolt was part of this Fourth Philosophy movement.

Apostle Paul
(5–67 C.E.?)

The earliest writings to be included in the New Testament were written by the Apostle Paul. Paul changed his name from Saul. Saul was born in Tarsus, a city in southern Asia Minor (what would now be in Turkey). Saul was born a Roman citizen (according to the book of Acts). He was a member of the Pharisees, was learned about the Hebrew Scripture, and spoke excellent Greek. He became a persecutor of the followers of Jesus. Three to five years after the death of Jesus, Saul had a life-changing experience. Saul was traveling to Damascus, the capital of Syria, to arrest followers of Jesus. There he had an experience where Jesus appeared to him and called him to be a follower and to become an apostle to the Gentiles. Although this experience is often referred to as a "conversion," it was a conversion from Pharisaic Judaism to Christian Judaism. After this conversion Saul came to be known as Paul. This event has become known as Paul's "Damascus experience," and it is interesting that this occurred a few years after the 40 days of appearances of Jesus that were reported in the book of Acts.

Other than Jesus, Paul is the most important figure in the New Testament. Some credit (or discredit) Paul with making Christianity a religion about Jesus rather than the religion of Jesus. His writings have had tremendous impact particularly on the theologian Augustine and for the Protestants during the Reformation. Thirteen of the 27 books of the New Testament have traditionally been attributed to him, and half of the book of Acts is about him. He is credited by some as the "founder of Christianity." Although 13 letters are attributed to Paul, only seven of them are undisputedly Pauline. Three are felt by scholars to be pseudonymous (not written by Paul), and three others are possibly pseudonymous. Ephesians, Colossians, and 2 Thessalonians are known as the "Deutero-Pauline" epistles. First Timothy, 2 Timothy, and Titus are known as the "Pastoral Epistles."

Undisputedly Pauline	**Possibly Paul**	**Likely Pseudonymous**
Romans	Ephesians	1 Timothy
1 Corinthians	Colossians	2 Timothy
2 Corinthians	2 Thessalonians	Titus
Galatians		
Philippians		
1 Thessalonians		
Philemon		

Pseudepigrapha

This term refers to texts where the author falsely attributes his writing to a figure from the past. We have already seen this in our examination of the books of the Hebrew Scripture. Many works had been falsely attributed to Solomon, son of David. Scholars know that forgeries were common in antiquity for a variety of reasons. Ancient authors themselves wrote about the frequency of forgeries. For some there was a profit motive, but for others the motive likely was less malevolent. For many of these writers the motive may have been to get important ideas out to the public. If they were to use their own name, likely no one would give any attention to their thoughts and ideas. If Solomon were to say it, however, that would be noteworthy! Also some authors may have tried to address problems and issues in the way they think their hero would have. This appears to be the case for the writer of "Paul's" third letter to the Corinthians, written after Paul's death to address some current problems in the church. This particular forger was "caught in the act."

The Period From 4 B.C.E. to 64 C.E.

This is the period from the time of Jesus' believed birth (4 B.C.E.) to the time of Paul's believed death (64 C.E.). Herod "the great" was made "king of the Jews" by the Romans in 40 B.C.E. and lived until 4 B.C.E., around the time of Jesus' birth. Herod was responsible for many building projects in Judea, including a fantastic expansion of the Jewish temple in Jerusalem. Upon his death, his kingdom was divided between his three sons: his son Herod Archelaus ruled Judea and Samaria, Herod Antipas ruled Galilee, and Herod Philip ruled the territories east of the Jordan. Herod "the Great," who was known to have been extremely ruthless, had previously executed three other sons (Alexander, Aristobulus, and Antipater) who were in the line of succession, believing that they planned to assassinate him.

Herod Archelaus ruled Judea only until 6 C.E. at which time he was banished to Gaul where he lived out his life. Judea then was governed by Roman prefects. Pontius Pilate was the prefect who governed from 26–30 C.E. It was likely that Herod Antipas was the Herod who played the role in the deaths of John the Baptist and Jesus.

Paul's letters

It was during this time period that the earliest books of the New Testament were written—the letters of the Apostle

Paul. It must be stressed that all of these were actual letters written by Paul to various churches and in one instance to an individual (Philemon). Paul did not know his writings eventually would be part of a Christian canon, and presumably there were other writings of Paul that were lost. The letters give us some information about Paul's theology, but we do not have a comprehensive treatise of his beliefs, although the letter to the Romans is the closest to this. The following is a list of Paul's letters and the most likely date of their composition:

1 Thessalonians	50 C.E.
Galatians	53 C.E.
1 Corinthians	54 C.E.
Philemon	55 C.E.
Philippians	55 C.E.
2 Corinthians	57 C.E.
Romans	58 C.E.

Paul's mission was to spread the "good news" of Jesus to the Gentiles. The other apostles focused on converting Jews in Palestine. Paul was an apocalypticist. He believed that there was a struggle in this age between the forces of good and evil. At the end of this age God would intervene and establish an age of justice and righteousness on earth. Paul believed that this would happen very soon—in his own lifetime. He believed that Jesus was the Son of God who was crucified by the Romans. He believed that Jesus rose from the dead and so defeated death. Paul saw this as the beginning of the new age, that Jesus would soon return to earth, and that all of the dead people who had ever lived would be raised from the dead as well to face judgment. Jesus' resurrection was the first sign of this new age, although the new age was not yet happening (but would be happening extremely soon).

Paul believed that the dietary laws and Jewish rituals were no longer necessary, especially for Gentiles. Jews and Gentiles were now both united as the people of God through Jesus Christ. The "orthodox" way of reading Paul is a concept known as "substitutionary atonement." The essence of this theology is that Jesus died as a sacrifice for the sins of mankind. It was the Jewish custom (as well as the custom of many surrounding cultures) to make animal sacrifices to God at the temple to make things right with God. The Old Testament book of Leviticus has detailed instructions on what offerings to make for various sins. Jesus was sacrificed by God to pay for all the sins of humanity. Jesus died in our place.

However, Christian scholars Marcus Borg and John Dominic Crossan do not believe this was Paul's belief. They write that the concept of "substitutionary atonement" originated in 1097 with a theological treatise by Anselm of Canterbury entitled *Cur Deus Homo*. Anselm maintained that forgiveness requires compensation, and none of us can afford that price that this would require. The death of Jesus, the incarnation of God, however, would cover the price. Borg and Crossan maintain that this would have been a very strange concept to Paul. Although Paul said that Jesus died for all people, Borg and Crossan maintain he was not talking about Jesus being a substitutionary sacrifice, but rather than he sacrificed his life for others in the same way that soldiers go to war and die "for their country." It is not to pay a price for their country's sins; it is a matter of sacrificing oneself for the welfare of others.

Borg and Crossan maintain that Christ's resurrection was of upmost importance to Paul, but so was the manner of Christ's death (i.e., being crucified by the Romans). It was the Roman Empire that killed Christ; Christ was perceived as a threat to the empire. Jesus challenged the domination system of the Romans. But Jesus was not defeated by death; he was resurrected, vindicated. Jesus was Lord—not Caesar.

Caesar Augustus was said to have been divine. He had been adopted by Julius Caesar who was officially recognized by the Roman senate as a god. Augustus was then known as "son of god." Augustus also was known as "god," "Lord," "Redeemer," and "Savior of the World." How did Augustus save the world? By defeating his enemies and uniting the Roman Republic. Augustus's reign was a period of peace known as the *Pax Romana* (Roman peace). The paradigm at that time throughout the world was that peace was the result of violent conquests.

Jesus, however, had a different formula for peace: a nonviolent path. Jesus said:

- Matt. 5:44 "Pray for those who persecute you."
- Luke 6:27–28 "Do good to those who hate you, bless those who curse you, pray for those who abuse you."
- Matt. 22:36–40 "He said to him, 'You shall love the Lord your God with all your heart, and with all your soul, and with all your mind.' This is the greatest and first commandment. And a second is like it: 'You shall love your neighbor as yourself.' On these two commandments hang all the law and the prophets."

Paul agrees with this philosophy:

- Rom. 12:14 "Bless those who persecute you; bless and do not curse them."
- Rom. 12:17 "Do not repay anyone evil for evil."
- Rom. 12:21 "Do not be overcome by evil, but overcome evil with good."
- Rom. 13:8–10 "Owe no one anything, except to love one another; for the one who loves another has fulfilled the law. The commandments, 'You shall not commit adultery; You shall not murder; You shall not steal; You shall not covet'; and any other commandment, are summed up in this word, 'Love your neighbor as yourself.' Love does no wrong to a neighbor; therefore, love is the fulfilling of the law."

It is not just the death and resurrection of Jesus that is important for Paul; it is the message of Jesus. That Jesus was resurrected from the dead demonstrates the superiority of Jesus over imperial Rome and the superiority of Jesus' paradigm of nonviolent justice over violent conquests. Borg and Crossan summarize it this way: "There will be peace on earth, said Roman imperial theology, when all is quiet and orderly. There will be peace on earth, said Pauline Christian theology, when all is fair and just."

There were systemic injustices in the world at that time, what Borg and others have termed "domination systems." Empires would dominate and subjugate people. In the case of the Jews, they were dominated by the Egyptians, the Babylonians, the Persians, the Greeks, and then the Romans. Many people were marginalized by those in power, for example, orphans, widows, slaves, and other people on the fringe of society. The powerful dominated the weak. Jesus and Paul challenged this system. "Do not be conformed to this world" says Paul (that is of injustice and violence); "but be transformed by the renewing of your minds, so that you may discern what is the will of God—what is good and acceptable and perfect" (Rom. 12:2).

Eschatology is theology about the final events of history. Jesus and Paul were both very focused on a "new age." But this new age would not be the destruction of the world but rather the end of an age of violence, oppression, and injustice. In the new age love would win.

The Period from 64 C.E. 100 C.E.

Both of the apostles Paul and Peter were believed to have died around 64 C.E. The period from 64 to 100 C.E. is the time period in which the Gospels were written. It also is a time period of much turmoil in Judea due to animosity toward a corrupt and dominating Roman Empire. Militant Jewish groups emerged, including a group known as the "Fourth Philosophy" or "The Zealots" who sought liberty from Roman rule. A rebellion broke out in 66 C.E.: It started out, according to the historian Josephus, as a simple refusal to continue prayers and sacrifices to the Roman emperor at the temple. There also were protests over taxation. In response to the unrest in Judea, Cestius Gallus led a Syrian legion to quell the rebellion. After several victories in the campaign, Gallus's troops were defeated by Judean rebels at the Battle of Beth Horon; this is often considered one of the worst military defeats the Romans suffered by a rebel province. Emperor Nero then sent Vespasian to lead three full Roman legions to suppress the uprising. By the fall of 67 C.E. Galilee had fallen to the Roman forces, and a year later

Judea also fell. The remaining rebels sought refuge in Jerusalem.

It was at this time period that Nero lost the support of the Roman Senate because of his erratic behaviors. Nero fled Rome and committed suicide. In 69 C.E. Vespasian became emperor and left his son, Titus, to finish the job of quelling the Judean uprisings. On Passover of the year 70 C.E. the Romans laid siege to Jerusalem. In August of that year the temple was destroyed. The Romans spread the news of this victory by minting coins with the inscription JUDAEA CAPTA, Judea has been captured.

Until then, the temple in Jerusalem had been the focus of Jewish worship. With the temple's destruction, synagogues became local centers of Jewish worship. Rabbis now replaced the role of high priest in Jewish society. Instead of sacrifice, prayer and the study of the Torah became central. This begins a period known as "Rabbinic Judaism." Rabbis achieved ordination based on learning and merit, whereas the priests had claimed their leadership because of birthright.

Gospel of Mark

It was during this period of time that the Christian gospels were written. I will discuss not only the four gospels that made it into the Christian canon, but other gospels that were written as well. The word "gospel" means good news, and it is a type of ancient religious biography, in our case about the life and teachings of Jesus of Nazareth. The gospel that was believed to have been written first is the Gospel According to Mark, which is believed to have been written about 70 C.E. It is the shortest of the gospels in the Christian canon.

This gospel has been historically attributed to John Mark, the secretary of the Apostle Peter, although we do not know who the actual author was. We do know it was written by a Greek speaking Christian about 35–40 years after Jesus' death. The author apparently heard stories about Jesus that had been circulating orally, and he wrote them down. Mark's gospel has no stories about Jesus' birth or early years, does not include the Lord's Prayer, and does not include many of Jesus' best known parables.

Mark's gospel's main message is to proclaim Jesus as the "Messiah." The first chapter of the book includes John the Baptist's proclamation of Jesus as being the fulfillment of the Jewish Scriptures, Jesus' baptism, and a voice coming down from heaven saying "You are my son, the Beloved, with you I am well pleased." From the beginning, Mark makes it clear that Jesus is the Messiah, the Son of God. This proclamation of Jesus as the Messiah would have been surprising to early readers who knew that Jesus of Nazareth had been crucified. The Jewish expectation for the coming Messiah would have been for a conquering figure of power that would defeat the forces of evil, not one killed and defeated himself! Mark makes the surprising point that not only is Jesus the Messiah despite his crucifixion, but that he is the Messiah *because* he suffered and died.

Already in the first chapter of Mark, Jesus begins his public ministry. Half of the gospel (chapters 1–8) narrates Jesus' activities in Galilee. Although he performs many miracles, nobody recognizes Jesus for what he is. In fact, Jesus tells his disciples to keep quiet about his identity. In chapter 8, verses 29–30 he asks them "But who do you say that I am?" Peter answered "You are the Messiah." "And he sternly ordered them not to tell anyone about him." This has become known as the "messianic secret." Throughout Mark's book Jesus tries to keep his identity a secret.

- Mark 1:34 "And he cured many who were sick with various diseases, and cast out many demons; and he would not permit the demons to speak, because they knew him."
- Mark 3:11–12 "Whenever the unclean spirits saw him, they fell down before him and shouted, 'You are the Son of God!' But he sternly ordered them not to make him known."
- Mark 1:42–43 "Immediately the leprosy left him, and he was made clean. After sternly warning him he sent him away at once, saying to him, 'See that you say nothing to anyone'."
- Mark 5:42–43 "And immediately the girl got up and began to walk about (she was twelve years of age). At this they were overcome with amazement. He strictly ordered them that no one should know this, and told them to give her something to eat."

For some Christians the key to gaining everlasting salvation and entry into heaven is the belief that Jesus is the Messiah. If this is true, why would Jesus try to keep this a secret?

Chapters 11–16, approximately 40% of the Book of Mark, tells the story of Jesus' final week of his life in Jerusalem. The week begins with Jesus' triumphal entry into Jerusalem, riding a donkey (Palm Sunday). On Monday he entered the temple in Jerusalem and drove out the money changers. On Tuesday scribes, priests, and elders tried without success to discredit him at the temple. On Wednesday Judas, one of his disciples, betrays him to the Roman authorities. Thursday is the day he shared a meal with his disciples (The Lord's

Supper) and was then arrested by the authorities. On Friday he was condemned to death and crucified. Saturday was the Sabbath and nothing happened on that day. On Sunday morning Mary Magdalene, Mary (the mother of Jesus), and Salome went to the tomb of Jesus to anoint the body with spices. When they got there, Jesus' body was not there. They were greeted by a white robed figure, presumably an angel, who told them that Jesus had been "raised" and that Jesus would be seen again in Galilee. "So they went out and fled from the tomb, for terror and amazement had seized them; and they said nothing to anyone, for they were afraid."

This is where Mark's gospel ends. Because this ending seemed unsatisfying to many, new endings were added in later centuries. A longer ending (verses 9–20) was added in the late second century. In this ending Jesus appears to Mary Magdalene, then to two disciples who were walking in the country, and then to the eleven disciples. A shorter ending (to replace this longer addition) was added in the fourth century.

As I previously mentioned, it is believed that the Gospel of Mark was written about 70 C.E. It also might be remembered that an immensely important event occurred at this same time—the destruction of the temple of Jerusalem. This was a catastrophic event. After all, this was the dwelling place of God, a magnificent fortress, the only place where sacrifices were made to God. God had promised to dwell there forever. A major theme of Mark's gospel is the expectation that this age will be ending soon, and a new age will begin with the second coming of Jesus. This was anticipated by the writer of Mark to be soon, as it was thought by the Apostle Paul. "Truly I tell you, there are some standing here who will not taste death until they see that the kingdom of god has come with power" (Mark 9:1). This idea that a new age will soon be here is known as "imminent eschatology." Although this is a belief of the writer of Mark and the Apostle Paul, we do not know if this was Jesus' belief.

Quelle (Q)

Although the Gospel of Mark is the earliest *narrative* account we have of the life of Jesus, there is believed to be an even earlier writing that gives us sayings of Jesus, the hypothetical book known as Quelle or Q. The word "quelle" comes from the German word for "source." It is hypothetical because we have not discovered this actual book. The reason it is believed to have existed, however, is that there are passages in both Mathew and Luke that are so identical that they must have come from the same source. It would be like reading articles about an event in two different newspapers; each article contains paragraphs that are word for word the same. The reason is that both articles are using portions taken from the Associated Press.

There are a lot of similarities between three of the gospels: Mark, Matthew, and Luke. They are called the "Synoptic Gospels." Both Matthew and Luke appear to have had access to both Mark and Q and used these sources in the composition of their gospels. Both Matthew and Luke also added other information in their gospels that was not part of Mark or Q. Thus there appears to have been four sources that contributed to the Synoptic Gospels:

- Mark
- Q

- "M" for Mathew's special source
- "L" for Luke's special source

Some of the most important and memorable passages in the gospels appear to have come from Q. These include:

- The Beatitudes
- The command to love one's enemies
- The command not to judge others
- The Lord's Prayer

Gospel of Matthew

The Gospel of Matthew is believed to have been written a decade or two after the Gospel of Mark. It is named after a disciple of Jesus, Matthew, the former tax collector. However, it is not believed by biblical scholars to have been written by Jesus' disciple. Names were not assigned to the gospels until the second century. The gospel itself is not claimed to be written by one of Jesus' disciples. Also, the fact that it is believed to have been written around the 80s or 90s makes it highly unlikely that it was written by a contemporary of Jesus. Also, it appears very likely that the author of Matthew used the Gospel of Mark as a source; why would an actual eyewitness to events do this?

The Book of Matthew is an expanded version of Mark. Ninety percent of Mark is in Matthew with the addition of stories about Jesus' birth, Jesus' teachings (much of which comes from Q), and some parables and sayings that are unique only to Matthew's gospel, e.g., that parable of the weed. The focus of Matthew is to portray Jesus as the new Moses. The gospel begins with a genealogy of Jesus. In

Matthew's genealogy there are 14 generations between each significant event of Jewish history:

- Fourteen generations between Abraham and David
- Fourteen generations between David and the deportation of the Jewish people to Babylon
- Fourteen generations between the deportation and Jesus, the Messiah

There are a few problems with Matthew's genealogy, however:

1. Matthew's genealogy is different from that in the Hebrew Scriptures (Chronicles).
2. Matthew's genealogy differs from the genealogy in Luke.
3. In trying to show that Jesus is from the line of David, Matthew provides the genealogy of Joseph. But Joseph was not Jesus' biological father, as Matthew reports that Mary, Jesus' mother, was a virgin.

Matthew goes to great lengths to demonstrate that Jesus is the fulfillment of the Jewish Scriptures. As predicted by the prophet Micah he was born in Bethlehem. As predicted by the prophet Isaiah, he was born of a virgin. Most importantly, Jesus is portrayed as the new Moses. All of this occurs only in Matthew's gospel. These are the parallels between Moses and Jesus according to Matthew:

- In the book of Exodus, the pharaoh orders that every Hebrew boy born should be killed and only the females should be allowed to live. When the infant Moses was born he was protected from harm. In

Matthew's gospel, Herod, the king of the Jews, kills all the children in and around Bethlehem who are two years old or younger in an attempt to kill the prophesized messiah. The infant Jesus escapes this by being brought to Egypt where he, like Moses, was protected.

- Moses passes through the waters of the Red (or Reed) Sea. Jesus passes through the waters of baptism.
- The children of Israel spend 40 years wandering in the desert wilderness. Jesus spends 40 days in the wilderness fasting and being tempted.
- Moses went up Mount Sinai where God delivers the Ten Commandments. Jesus also went up in the mountain and then delivered the Sermon on the Mount. Jesus said "Do not think I have come to abolish the law or the prophets; I have come not to abolish but to fulfill."

Jesus, as the new Moses, criticizes the Pharisees (chapter 23) for focusing on picayune, unimportant matters and neglecting "the weightier matters of the law: justice and mercy and faith." "You blind guides! You strain out a gnat but swallow a camel!" In the Sermon on the Mount are some statements by Jesus known as the "six antitheses." In these statements Jesus does not overturn the laws of Moses but clarifies and expands upon them. Jesus said that not only are we not to murder, but we are not to show hatred. Not only are we not to commit adultery, but we are not to show lechery. Instead of repaying an eye for an eye, we are to turn the other cheek. Instead of hating our enemies, we are to love them. Jesus summarized the law as being first "love the Lord your God with all your heart" and secondly "Love your neighbor as yourself" (Matt. 22:36–40). This originally comes from the Hebrew Scripture:

- Deut. 6:5 "You shall love the Lord your God with all your heart, and with all your soul, and with all your might."
- Lev. 19:18 "You shall not take vengeance or bear a grudge against any of your people, but you shall love your neighbor as yourself: I am the Lord."

Unlike in the Gospel of Mark where Jesus is reluctant to let people know who he is, in Matthew Jesus is openly recognized as the messiah in his lifetime.

Gospel of Luke

Most biblical scholars date the composition of the Gospel According to Luke at around the same time as Matthew, around 85 C.E. A few scholars date it even later at around 110 C.E. It was written in Greek. Although we call the author "Luke," it was written anonymously. Like Matthew's gospel, Luke includes a genealogy of Jesus, although Luke's goes all the way back to Adam stressing Jesus' relationship not only with Jews but with all of mankind. Matthew's gospel emphasizes the Jewishness of Jesus by demonstrating Jesus' line of descent from Abraham the father of the Jews and David, king of the Jews. Luke wants to demonstrate Jesus' commonality with all people. Like Matthew's genealogy, Jesus' pedigree is demonstrated through Jesus' "adopted" father, Joseph. However, the two genealogies are different. In Matthew Jesus is descended from King David's son, Solomon. In Luke Jesus is descended from King David's son, Nathan.

Also like Matthew, in Luke there are stories about Jesus' birth (Mark and John do not discuss Jesus' birth). The two accounts are very different, however. In both Jesus is born in Bethlehem to the Virgin Mary, although in Matthew's account the intimation is that the family lived in Bethlehem, and in Luke's account the family travels from Nazareth to Bethlehem to register for a census. However, there is no historical evidence for such censuses to have taken place, and it particularly would make no sense for people to return to their *ancestral* home for a census. "Joseph also went from the town of Nazareth in Galilee to Judea, to the city of David called Bethlehem, because he was descended from the house and family of David" (Luke 2:4). David lived a thousand years earlier. Would you know where to register for a census if you had to go to the home of an ancestor who lived 1,000 years earlier?

When we hear the birth story of Jesus now, it is a conflation of the two accounts of Matthew and Luke. In Matthew's account an angel of the Lord appears to Joseph in a dream and tells him to take Mary as his wife and that she is pregnant with a child conceived through the Holy Spirit, who should be named Jesus. Joseph "did as the angel of the Lord commanded him; he took her as his wife, but had no marital relations with her until she had borne a son; and he named him Jesus" (Matt. 1:24–25). The birth occurs in their hometown of Bethlehem. There is no story of a manger or shepherds. There is a story of three wise men (not kings), however. To escape Herod, who wants to kill the child who has been born "king of the Jews," the family goes to Egypt and stays there until Herod's death. Then because of fears about Herod's son and successor Archelaus, the family moves to Nazareth rather than returning to Bethlehem.

Luke's story of Jesus' birth is much different from Matthew's. An angel of the Lord (Gabriel) comes to Mary, not Joseph. "And now, you will conceive in your womb and bear a son, and you will name him Jesus" (Luke 1:31). In Luke the family lives in Nazareth and travels to Bethlehem to register for the census. There Mary gives birth; because "there was no place for them in the inn" Mary lays Jesus in a manger. Shepherds who are watching their flock by night are approached by an angel who tells them of Jesus' birth. They travel to Bethlehem to see baby Jesus. Luke then tells of Jesus' circumcision eight days later and then of his presentation to the Lord at the temple in Jerusalem ("as it is written in the law of the Lord, 'Every firstborn male shall be designated as holy to the Lord,' and they offered a sacrifice according to what is stated in the law of the Lord, 'a pair of turtledoves or two young pigeons.'")

Although there are contradictions between the two accounts, one should not think of the gospels as being histories in the modern sense. The writers of the gospels took stories and sayings of Jesus that had been spread by word of mouth and formulated their gospels to tell a deeper "truth." I have had people tell me from time to time that they do not like to read fiction because it is not "true." But just because something is not factually true, it does not mean that it can't relate a deeper truth. A good example is Jesus' parables. Jesus is not telling stories about actual events that occurred; he is telling stories that he made up that tell a deeper truth. Marcus Borg and John Crossan put it well in their book, *The First Christmas: What the Gospels Really Teach About Jesus's Birth* (2007). The themes expressing these truths include:

- "What is the 'King of the Jews'? That was Herod the Great's title, but Matthew's story tells us Herod was more like pharaoh, the lord of Egypt, the lord of bondage and oppression, violence and brutality. And his son was no better. Rather, Jesus is the true King of the Jews. And the rulers of his world sought to destroy him."

- "Who is the Son of God, Lord, savior of the world, and the one who brings peace on earth? Within Roman imperial theology, the emperor, Caesar, was all of these. No, Luke's story says, that status and those titles belong to Jesus. He—not the emperor—is the embodiment of God's will for the earth."

- "Who is the light of the world? The emperor, son of Apollo, the god of light and reason and imperial order? Or is Jesus, who was executed by empire, the light in the darkness, the true light to whom the wise of this world are drawn?"

- "Where do we find the fulfillment of God's dream for Israel and humanity? In the way things are now? Or only beyond death? Or in a very different world this side of death?"

The same is true of the accounts of Jesus' death on the cross. Again when we hear of the seven last words of Christ on the cross, this is a conflation of the accounts of Matthew, Mark, Luke, and John. Mark's portrayal of Jesus on the cross is much different than Luke's. In Mark, although Jesus foretells his death and resurrection three times, when the time is getting close he prays three times in Gethsemane "that, if it were possible, the hour might pass from him. He said, 'Abba, Father, for you all things are possible; remove this cup from me; yet, not what I want, but what you want'" (Mark 14:35–36). When Jesus is on the cross, he is silent throughout the whole ordeal until the end when he cries out in a loud voice "'Eloi, Eloi, lema sabachthani?' which means, 'My God, my God, why have you forsaken me?'" (Mark 15:34). The portrayal of Jesus' death in Luke is much different. Jesus is confidant and without doubts. On the way to his crucifixion Jesus expresses concern about the women who are weeping for him and is not concerned about his own fate. On the cross he prays for those who are crucifying him: "Father, forgive them; for they do not know what they are doing" (Luke 23:34). He says to the repentant criminal on the cross next to him "Truly I tell you, today you will be with me in Paradise" (Luke 23:43). In Mark, Jesus is in agony and apparent doubt. In Luke, Jesus dies with calm and confidence.

In Luke, Jesus is portrayed as a prophet such as Elijah, Elisha, and, particularly, Samuel. Instead of an emphasis on Jesus being the *Jewish* messiah, the importance of Jesus to the entire world is stressed. The "good news" must also be shared with the Gentiles. To spread the gospel to the world will take some time, and so the end of the age is not portrayed as being imminent in Luke, as it is in Mark, Matthew and the writings of Paul. Also in Luke the "kingdom of God" has already come:

> "Once Jesus was asked by the Pharisees when the kingdom of God was coming, and he answered, 'The kingdom of God is not coming with things that can be observed; nor will they say, "Look, here it is!" or "There it is!" For, in fact, the kingdom of God is among you.'" (Luke 17:20–21)

Because it will take some time for the end of the age, there is a stronger emphasis in Luke than Mark and Matthew on a social agenda (i.e., hunger, poverty, oppression, justice).

There is a need to address these issues if the end is not imminent.

The Acts of the Apostles

Although not a "gospel," the book of Acts is included here because it is really the second volume of the writings of "Luke." Biblical scholars are convinced it was written by the same author as the Gospel of Luke. This is the only composition in the New Testament canon to tell the story of the apostles after the death of Jesus and the story of the very early church. The title, "Acts of the Apostles," is a bit of a misnomer as most of the apostles are never talked about in the book. It primarily tells the story of Peter and in particular Paul. The Holy Spirit is also one of the major characters of this book. Acts begins by informing the reader that after Jesus' death on the cross Jesus appeared to the apostles for 40 days, teaching them about the kingdom. Then he ascended into heaven: "a cloud took him out of their sight."

Matthias is chosen as an apostle to replace Judas Iscariot. On the day of Pentecost (which is a day on the Jewish calendar celebrating the giving of the law on Mt. Sinai) the Holy Spirit came upon the apostles. For Christians, Pentecost is now known as the "birthday of the church" rather than being known for its earlier Jewish significance. Thousands of Jews converted as a result of the apostles' teachings. However, most Jews continued to reject the gospel. For this reason, God now offers the good news to the Gentiles. In chapter 8 of Acts, Philip preaches to the Samaritans, and many convert. The Apostle Peter has a vision in which he learns from God that Gentiles are to be preached the good news.

Peter preaches to the Gentiles who then receive the Holy Spirit.

One famous Jew who converts is Saul, also known as Paul. The Acts of the Apostles tells the story of Paul's conversion experience on the road to Damascus, after which he becomes an apostle. Paul in particular was instrumental in spreading the gospel to Gentiles. Acts describes three missionary journeys of Paul throughout Syria, Asia Minor (modern-day Turkey), Macedonia, and Achaia (modern-day Greece). From chapter 13 to the end of the book, Acts describes the missionary work of Paul.

Acts also talks about another major event in the early Christian church, an event which occurred around 50 C.E. It was a meeting between Paul and the other apostles and is now known as the Jerusalem Council. The question was whether Gentile converts had to become "Jewish" first. Of particular importance was the question of circumcision. Paul's views prevailed, and it was decided that Gentiles did not need to observe all of the Jewish laws, e.g., males did not need to be circumcised.

There are a number of discrepancies between Paul's actual accounts of events and the accounts of events given by the author of Luke, who is writing decades later. Just a few of the many examples include:

- In Galatians, Paul said that after his conversion he waited three years before going to Jerusalem to meet the other apostles. Acts has him going to Jerusalem right away.
- According to Paul it was on his second trip to Jerusalem in which the Jerusalem Council (to

determine the necessity of circumcision for Gentiles) occurred; according to Acts it was his third trip there.

- Paul himself does not make claims of being a miracle worker, but Acts has him performing many miracles such as curing blindness, raising a young man from the dead, etc.
- Paul reports that he's a good writer but a poor orator; Acts describes him as an eloquent orator.

And so the book of Acts appears to be a very inaccurate historical document (if one is to assume that Paul was an accurate reporter of his own life). However, like the Gospels, the purpose of Luke's book was to make theological points, not to relate history in the modern sense. Luke's main points are to proclaim that the apostles and early Christians were empowered by the Holy Spirit, that the good news was meant for the Gentiles and not just the Jews, that the good news spread throughout the world and to many different peoples, that this was God's plan from the beginning, and that converts did not have to become Jewish first (or be circumcised) in order to become Christians.

The Gospel of John

Like the other gospels, John was written anonymously. Although tradition ascribes the book to John, the son of Zebedee, one of Jesus' disciples, biblical scholars are confidant it was not. As with the other gospels in the canon, the author does not name himself. It was not believed to have been ascribed to the disciple John until the end of the second century. Also John was said to have been illiterate. "Now when they saw the boldness of Peter and John and realized that they were uneducated and ordinary men, they were amazed and recognized them as companions of Jesus" (Acts 4:13). John is believed by scholars to have been written around 90–95 C.E., likely the last of the four gospels of the canon to have been written.

John is very much different from the gospels of Mark, Matthew and Luke (known together as the Synoptic Gospels). There are many stories in John not found in the Synoptic Gospels, and many of the well-known stories of the other three gospels are not found in John, including stories about Jesus' birth, his baptism, his preaching about the coming kingdom of God, casting out demons, any parables, the transfiguration before some of the disciples, and institution of the Lord's Supper.

John tells us that Jesus existed along with God, the Father, since the beginning of time. Only in John, the last of the gospels to be written, is Jesus unambiguously God. Some of Jesus' most amazing miracles happen in John including turning water into wine and raising Lazarus from the dead. Unlike the other gospels where Jesus is quite reticent about letting others know about his miraculous acts, in John proclaiming his identity appears to be the main reason he does them. They are "signs" that demonstrate to people his power. Unlike the other gospels, he does not preach about the coming of the kingdom of God on earth. Rather, his emphasis is on himself as being "the light of the world" and "the resurrection and the life." "I am the way, the truth, and the life. No one comes to the Father except through me" (John 14:6).

James

Unlike the Gospels, the author of the letter of James specifically names himself as "James," although he does not say which James he is. Tradition has it that he is the James who is the brother of Jesus, who was the leader of the church in Jerusalem. If this were true, it likely would be the earliest writing included in the New Testament canon (then likely being written in the 40s or 50s). However, it is very doubtful that this really was written by the James who was Jesus' brother. That James was a lower-class peasant from rural Galilee who spoke Aramaic. It is very doubtful that he would be writing an eloquently written letter in Greek. Most scholars date the letter of James to anywhere from the 70s to the early 100s. The "letter" was not addressed to a particular person or group but rather appears to have been moral exhortations to Christian Jews in general. The letter may have been written to oppose the views of Paul. Whereas Paul wrote, "For we hold that a person is justified by faith apart from works prescribed by the law" (Rom. 3:28); James wrote, "You see that a person is justified by works and not by faith alone. . . . For just as the body without the spirit is dead, so faith without works is also dead" (James 2:24, 26).

James is critical of the rich and of those who give favoritism to the rich. He complains that laborers are not paid adequately. He says that simply knowing Jesus is not enough but that we have to put love in action. "Even the demons believe—and shudder" (James 2:19). Simply believing is not enough for James.

The letter of James has generated some controversy through the ages. Martin Luther, who strongly believed in Paul's concept of "justification by grace through faith," wanted to have the book removed from the New Testament canon.

Epistle to the Hebrews

The name of this book really is a misnomer; it is not an epistle or letter, and it is not written to Hebrews or Jews. At one time attributed to the Apostle Paul, Paul's name appears nowhere in the book, and the writing style has no similarities to Paul's. Scholars are convinced it was not written by Paul. It is believed to have been a sermon written to a Christian congregation discouraging congregants from leaving the Christian church and becoming Jewish. The writing is a "word of exhortation" about the superiority of Christianity to Judaism. "Long ago God spoke to our ancestors in many and various ways by the prophets, but in these last days he has spoken to us by a Son, whom he appointed heir of all things, through whom he also created the worlds" (Heb. 1:1–2). The writer explains Christ's superiority to the angels, to Moses, and to the Hebrew prophets. Jesus was the ultimate high priest who made the supreme sacrifice of himself. There is some irony that the religion of Jesus, who never meant to start a new religion and taught as a Jew, was now being denigrated by some of his followers. Some consider this book one of the earliest writings of the Christian church's movement toward anti-Semitism.

Revelation

The Book of Revelation is arguably the most controversial book in the Bible. It was written by a man named "John" (writing from the Island of Patmos) who some in history have thought was John, the disciple. Biblical scholars do not think so. They also do not think it was written by the same author who wrote the Gospel of John. It was believed to have been written in the 90s. There was some reluctance, particularly by the Eastern Church, to include it in the New Testament canon.

I discussed earlier in this book the genre of apocalypses. These are writings that were popular for both Jews and Christians of that time and centuries earlier. They are revelations, often described as dreams or visions, in which the world is described in the dichotomy of good and evil. They use highly symbolic language in describing both the oppression and suffering of the present world and a coming age in which judgment is imposed on the evil doers and the righteous are blessed. In times of distress, these writings give hope that God will intervene and make things right in the end. These writings were quite popular, and two other examples of apocalypses around this time included the Shepherd of Hermas and the Apocalypse of Peter. Earlier Jewish apocalypses included writings purportedly written by Moses, Abraham, Enoch, and even Adam.

The concept that the present age was about to end and that a new age of righteousness would begin has been common throughout history. Many early Christians thought the end of this age was very near (i.e., in their generation). Paul discouraged marriage due to the coming of the ending of this age. Many Christians thought the end of the world was coming at the end of the first millennium (1000 C.E.). Pope Innocent III identified the rise of Islam as the reign of the Antichrist, who he identified as Muhammad. Using Revelation as his guide he predicted the second coming as being in 1284 (666 years after the founding of Islam).

Reformers Martin Luther and John Wesley predicted that the second coming was near. Joseph Smith, the founder of the Mormon Church, thought the second coming would come when he was 85 years old; he died when he was 38 in 1844. Throughout the ages, hundreds of "prophets" have predicted an imminent second coming. None of them have been right. A literal interpretation of the symbolic imagery found in the Book of Revelation (known as millennialism) continues to be a popular talking-point for televangelists and fundamentalist churches. The Catholic Church and mainline Protestant churches have primarily held an amillennial position (meaning not a literal interpretation). The recently published series of books known as the "Left Behind" series which ascribes to millennialism has sold millions of copies.

The prevailing view of the Book of Revelation is that the author is writing about the oppression that is occurring in his own time. The "whore of Babylon" in the book is Rome. Contemporary readers to John of Patmos would have readily recognized Rome as the "great city that rules over the kings of the earth," that has seven heads (the well-known city built on seven hills), and the persecutor of Christians. The antichrist in chapter 13 is given the number "666." A common practice at that time was to assign numerical values to letters. If we were to spell Caesar Nero's name in Hebrew letters and add them up, the total would be 666. Nero was the Roman emperor at that time, a persecutor of Christians, the leader of an empire that dominated and oppressed the people of Palestine. The writer of Revelation wrote to give hope to the people of that time that God was in control and that the forces of good would triumph over evil. However, he expected this to happen soon; it did not.

First Clement

This is a letter that was not included in the New Testament but was written very early, in the late first century C.E. It was written from the Roman Christians to the Corinthian church to address perceived problems in the Corinthian church. The letter gives guidelines for church governance. The letter describes apostolic succession, i.e., the apostles were chosen by Christ, and the church leaders were chosen by the apostles. There is evidence it was used as Scripture by the Corinthians around 170 C.E. and was considered part of the New Testament in some regions.

The Roman Period
(100 to 200 C.E.)

In the second century of the Common Era, a number of other writings were composed that were used as Scripture, although most were not adopted for the New Testament canon. This was a period of continuing animosity by Jews and Christians toward the Romans. A very significant event occurred from 132–136 C.E. in Judea, known as the Bar Kokhba revolt. Simon bar Kokhba was the man who led the revolt, and he was thought by many Jews at that time to be the promised Messiah. You might remember that in 70 C.E. the Romans destroyed the Jewish temple as a result of a war between the Jews and the Romans. Tensions continued to be high and reached a boiling point when circumcision (seen to be mutilation by the Romans) was outlawed, and a temple honoring Jupiter was planned to be built on the site of the destroyed temple of Yahweh.

The revolt was crushed in the summer of 135, and there were massive casualties for both the Jews and the Romans. This was the end of Judea as an entity; it was merged into Syria Palaestina. Hadrian, the Roman emperor, then forbade the practices of the Jewish faith. Jerusalem was renamed Aelia Capitolina. Jews became a minority in Judea. The majority of the Jewish population were killed or exiled, and Babylon became the new center of the Jewish community.

There was not widespread persecution of Christians at this time, although in the earliest history of Christianity many did not understand it and there were rumors of many deviant and bizarre practices, such as cannibalism (eating the body and blood of Christ) and incest (the Christian references to each other as "brother and sister"). As Christianity became better understood, these rumors subsided. Although Romans generally were open and tolerant of various religious beliefs, they were leery about people who did not participate in the public worship of the pagan gods. In other words, it was not a problem that Yahweh and Jesus were worshipped, but it was a problem that the pagan gods also were not worshipped.

Remaining Books in the New Testament Canon

There were some other writings that are included in the New Testament canon that were written between 100 and 120 C.E. These include letters that were at one time attributed to the Apostle Paul but are now thought to have been written by someone else. These letters include the possibly pseudonymous letters of **Ephesians, Colossians** (which may have been written earlier around 85 C.E.), and **2**

Thessalonians, and the highly likely pseudonymous letters of **1 and 2 Timothy** and **Titus**.

Likely dates:

Paul's death	64 C.E.
Colossians	80s C.E.
Ephesians	90s C.E.
2 Thessalonians	100 C.E.
1 and 2 Timothy	110s C.E.
Titus	10s C.E.

Two of the major criticisms leveled against Paul have been his stand on women and slavery. However, the objectionable passages come from 1 and 2 Timothy and Titus, not from undisputed actual letters from Paul. In regards to slavery, in Titus the writer says "Tell slaves to be submissive to their masters and to give satisfaction in every respect; they are not to talk back, not to pilfer, but to show complete and perfect fidelity, so that in everything they may be an ornament to the doctrine of God our Savior" (Titus 2:9–10). Yet the Paul of the Letter to Philemon shows a much more compassionate person who encourages his Christian brother Philemon to take back his slave, Onesimus, not as a slave but as a "beloved brother."

In regards to the role of women, in the genuine letters of Paul he presents as quite egalitarian. Although he says that wives have responsibilities to their husbands, he also says that husbands have equal responsibilities to wives. He talks about many women who are active and leaders in the early Christian church including "our sister, Phoebe, a deacon of the church at Cenchreae" (Rom. 16:1). In this same chapter of Romans, Paul goes on to praise other members of the church, 10 of the 27 mentioned as being women. Junia, one of those mentioned, was said to be "prominent among the apostles." In contrast, the writer of the letter to Timothy says:

> Let a woman learn in silence with full submission. I permit no woman to teach or to have authority over a man; she is to keep silent. For Adam was formed first, then Eve; and Adam was not deceived, but the woman was deceived and became a transgressor. Yet she will be saved through childbearing, provided they continue in faith and love and holiness, with modesty. (Tim. 2:11–15)

Also from this period are three writings known as the Johannine epistles: **1, 2,** and **3 John**. These writings come from the same community that produced the Gospel of John. They were not written by the Apostle John, and neither do scholars believe they were written by the author of the Gospel of John. There is a dispute about whether the same author wrote all three of the epistles. They were written around 100 C.E. or slightly later. **1 John** really is not a letter, although **2** and **3 John** are. Both 1 and 2 John expressed concerns about "deceivers" who believe that Jesus was only divine and did not come in the flesh. This belief came to be known as "docetism."

The remaining books of the New Testament canon that I have not yet discussed are **Jude** and **1 and 2 Peter**. Jude calls himself "a servant of Jesus Christ and a brother of James." Early traditions about Jesus included the belief that he had brothers, and two of them were named James and Jude (or Judas), both very common names at that time. So for a long time it was thought that Jude who wrote this letter was the brother of Jesus and James. Many scholars now believe it was not and was written much later, around 100 C.E. The letter contains condemnations about "intruders" in the community who "pervert the grade of our God." Scholars believe that the author of 2 Peter was familiar with Jude and incorporated portions of it. Second Peter is believed to be the latest book in the New Testament canon to have been written, likely 120 to 150 C.E. There is certainty in the belief of scholars that it was not written by the apostle Peter. Nor was 1 Peter believed to have been written by the apostle (or by the writer of 2 Peter). First Peter was most likely written around Rome between 90 and 110 C.E. It is only one of two writings in the canon that uses the word "Christian" (the other is Acts). The book addresses the issue of persecution of early Christians. Although it was not illegal to be a Christian, there was some local (not state) persecution of Christians at this time. This was not because of their belief in Jesus as the Christ, but rather because of their refusal to worship the state gods. The writer of 1 Peter tells readers to expect to suffer but to continue to do what is good.

Nag Hammadi Library

In 1945 in Egypt some peasants uncovered a jar that contained 13 documentary fragments that were written in Coptic, an ancient Egyptian language. The books were produced in the mid-fourth century, but they are of writings that we know existed in the second century (as they are mentioned in writings that continued to exist). So with this discovery we were able to finally learn what was in these books. The reason they were not to be found for centuries is that the "proto-orthodox" faction of Christianity destroyed them. The Nag Hammadi library represents a faction of Christianity back then known as "gnostic." Some of these writings will be discussed below. The term "proto-orthdodox" is used to describe the form of Christianity endorsed by some Christians of the second and third centuries, particularly the Roman church. This form of Christianity eventually "won out" over competing theologies.

Other Gospels

There are many Christian gospels that did not make it into the New Testament canon. Matthew, Mark, Luke, and John do appear to be the earliest written gospels that we have, although they all were written long after Jesus lived and died. There likely were earlier written narratives of Jesus, however, that did not survive. Luke at the beginning of his gospel notes that "many have undertaken to set down an orderly account of the events" including from eyewitnesses. Here are some other gospels that have survived to this day that did not make it into the canon, although were considered "Scripture" by many early Christian communities. Many were discovered only in the past century.

The Gospel of Thomas

This is not a narrative gospel but a collection of the sayings of Jesus (114 in all). It was discovered in the Nag Hammadi library in 1945 completely preserved. The author gives his name as Didymus Judas Thomas; this is the person many Syrian Christians believed was the twin brother of Jesus. It was probably written in the early second century, although some scholars have dated it as early as 50 C.E. More than half of the sayings in the Gospel of Thomas can be found in the Synoptic Gospels, and so many of the other sayings are novel to modern ears. Most of the verses begin with "Jesus said." This book does not mention Jesus' miracles, death, or crucifixion; what matters in this book are the teachings of Jesus. A primary emphasis is a description of what Jesus said about the coming kingdom of God.

- "Jesus said, 'If your leaders say to you, "Look, the kingdom is in the sky," then the birds of the sky will precede you. If they say to you, "It is in the sea," then the fish will precede you. But the kingdom is within you, and it is outside you. When you come to know yourselves, then you will be known, and you will understand that you are the children of the living Father. But if you will not know yourselves, then you are in poverty, and it is you who are the poverty.'" (Thomas 3)
- "His disciples said to him, 'When will the kingdom come?' 'It will not come by waiting for it. It will not be said, 'Look, here it is,' or 'Look, it is there.' Rather, the kingdom of the Father is spread out upon the earth, and people do not see it." (Thomas 113)

The Gospel of Judas Iscariot

This gospel was likely written in the middle of the second century; it was known to Irenaeus writing in 180 C.E., but it has not been known to readers since that time until it was discovered in 1978 south of Cairo in Egypt. It focuses on Jesus' last days on earth, and in this gospel Judas is not the villain but is working on behalf of Jesus. Judas is the disciple who is most superior. Jesus tells him: "You will exceed all of them, for you will sacrifice the man that clothes me."

Jesus' death allows Jesus to leave his bodily shell which has entrapped his spiritual self. It is not the death of Jesus which brings salvation. In this gospel there is no physical resurrection of Jesus' body; the body is perceived as evil.

The Gospel of Peter

This gospel was known to Eusebius, and thus its existence was known throughout the ages, although it was not available to modern readers until 1886 when a fragment of it was found in a grave in Egypt. It was popular in some Christian communities in the second century, particularly in some parts of Syria. Supposedly it was written by the disciple Peter, and Jesus' burial was described in the first person: "We fasted and sat mourning and crying night and day until the Sabbath" (v. 27). Herod is responsible for Jesus' death in this gospel rather than Pontius Pilate. This gospel includes an account of Jesus' resurrection and emergence from his tomb. The stone to the tomb rolls away on its own, and three men emerge whose heads reach to the heavens. They are followed by a cross. From heaven comes a voice: "Have you preached to those who are sleeping?" It is the cross that replies with "yes" (vv.41–42).

Infancy Gospel of Thomas

This gospel was discovered near Nag Hammadi and has been dated as early as 125 C.E. It tells the story of Jesus as a child, from the ages of five until 12 when he was teaching in the temple. The book starts with a story of Jesus at the age of five making birds out of clay on the Sabbath; he is chastised by someone who sees him and then by his father, Joseph, for profaning the Sabbath. Jesus responds by clapping his hands, making the birds come to life. They fly off chirping.

As a child, Jesus has a very bad temper. In one incident "a child ran up and banged into his shoulder. Jesus was aggravated and said to him, 'You will go no further on your way.' Right away the child fell down and died." As time goes on, however, Jesus matures and starts to use his supernatural powers for good.

The Proto-Gospel of James

There were many infancy gospels written particularly after the second century C.E. One likely from the second century, however, is the Proto-Gospel of James. It was known to Origen in the third century and became popular in later centuries. It is called "proto" because it narrates events primarily that happened prior to Jesus' birth. It was assumed to have been written by Jesus' stepbrother, James. The book focuses a great deal on Mary, whose own birth was miraculous: she was conceived by an older woman, Anna, who was barren. Mary conceives Jesus through the Holy Spirit. Not only is she a virgin when she becomes pregnant, but even after delivering Jesus she is a virgin: she is inspected by the midwife, Salome, and is found to be "intact."

The Gospel of Mary

Large portions of this gospel were first discovered in 1896, but they were not published until 1955. Its central character is Mary Magdalene. It was probably written in the mid to late second century. In the latter part of the book Mary Magdalene tells the disciples a revelation that Jesus told her and not them. Peter questions this and then is rebuked by Levi: "If the Savior made her worthy, who are you then, for your part, to cast her aside? Surely the Savior knows her full well. That is why he has loved her more than us."

Apocalypse of Peter

This was discovered in Egypt in 1886 and likely was written in the early second century. It was claimed to have been written by the apostle, Peter. In it Jesus gives a description of the last judgment, the torments of hell, and the blessings of those who are saved.

The Coptic Apocalypse of Peter

This apocalypse, also allegedly written by the apostle Peter, was discovered at Nag Hammadi. Scholars believe it was likely written in the third century. In this book Peter records visions that Jesus had. Jesus warns against the false teachings that he literally died on the cross and that it was his death that was important. Jesus teaches that the crucifixion provided release of Jesus from his physical shell. He was put into the fleshly body only in order to be able to deliver important teachings. It is these teachings that bring salvation—not Jesus' death on the cross.

The Secret Book of John

This book also was discovered at Nag Hammadi and is a post-resurrection discussion between Jesus and the apostle John. Jesus teaches there is one great God who is illimitable, unfathomable, immeasurable, invisible, eternal, unutterable and unnamable. It was a lesser god who created the world and humankind. Jesus teaches the way for divine souls to leave the prisons of their earthly physical bodies.

Book of Thomas

This also was discovered at Nag Hammadi. Jesus calls the author "brother" and "twin and true friend." Part of the book is a dialogue between Jesus and Thomas, and the other part is a monologue by Jesus. A main theme of the book is the avoidance of bodily passions and the importance of the soul. It is important to escape the pains and passions of the body.

The Acts of Peter

This is an account of actions, sermons and miracles of the apostle, Peter. Many of these miracles are indeed fantastic!

> "And Peter turning around saw a smoked tuna fish hanging in a window. He took it, saying to the people, 'When you see this swimming in water like a fish, will you be able to believe in him whom I preach?' And all said with one voice, 'Indeed we shall believe you.' So he went to the pond near by, saying, 'In your name, O Jesus Christ, in whom they do not yet believe, I say, 'Tuna, in the presence of all

these, live and swim like a fish.' And he cast the tuna into the pond, and it became alive and began to swim. The multitude saw the swimming fish and he made it swim not only for that hour but, lest they said that it was a deception, he made it swim longer, thereby attracting crowds from all parts and showing that the smoked tuna had again become a living fish."

Peter also is able to make dogs and infants speak. He has contests with a magician known as Simon Magus, who presents himself also as a representative of God. Simon too can perform miracles. At one point he flies over Rome like a bird. Peter calls on God to smite him, and he falls to earth. This convinces the crowds of Peter's superior powers, and they stone Simon.

The Acts of Paul

Like "Luke's" book of Acts, this is an account of Paul's travels. There is one particularly remarkable tale in this book, however. In Ephesus Paul is thrown to the lions. He recognizes the lion that comes upon him as one he previously baptized. He asks the lion if he is the one, and the lion replies that he is. The governor then sends other beasts to attack Paul, but a violent hailstorm comes on that saves both Paul and the baptized lion.

The Acts of John

This is the story of the apostle John, the disciple Jesus was perhaps closest to. It describes many miracles that John performs. In Ephesus as a result of John's prayer ("May the deity of this place, which has deceived so many, now also give way to your name") a pagan temple fell to the ground, idols were destroyed, and pagan priests were killed. This leads to the conversion of many people.

The Acts of Thomas

As previously mentioned, Judas Thomas was allegedly Jesus' twin brother. This book was probably written in the early third century rather than the second. The account includes descriptions of both heaven and hell. There is one account in which a woman is raised from the dead; she had previously been in hell and describes her experiences.

The Didache

This book was written around 100 C.E. and is thus a very early Christian composition. It is an anonymous work which has three main sections: Christian lessons; rituals such as baptism, fasting, and the Eucharist; and church organization. There are 16 short chapters in the book. It was considered part of some early canons but did not eventually make it into the New Testament canon.

Epistle of Barnabas

This writing was attributed to Barnabas, the companion of the Apostle Paul. However, the author never identifies himself in the work. Scholars believe it was written around 130 C.E., perhaps in Alexandria. It was very popular in many Christian communities and was included in some canons. It is a very anti-Jewish book. The author argues that Judaism is a false religion and views much of the Hebrew Scripture as allegorical writings rather than being literally true. For example, the author argues that Jewish Scripture should not be interpreted literally to not eat pigs, but rather advocates an allegorical meaning, i.e., not to live like swine. The author does not believe the Jews were the "people of God."

The Shepherd of Hermas

This was written by a Christian named Hermas, and like The Epistle of Barnabas, was included in some church canons. It was written in the middle of the second century in Rome. It is apocalyptic writing and is divided into five visions, 12 sets of mandates, and 10 parables. The book is very concerned about baptized Christians who have lapsed into sin. Hermas maintains that these individuals have but one chance to repent. If they lapse yet again, there is no hope for them.

The Apostolic Fathers

The term "apostolic fathers" was given in the 17th century to a group of second-century writers who were second generation Christians, i.e., followers of Jesus' apostles. Their writings were considered authoritative by "proto-orthodox" Christians at that time (and still now), although they did not make it into the New Testament canon. These writers were:

- Barnabas (The Epistle of Barnabas, described above)
- Clement of Rome (I Clement: described above)
- Hermas (The Shepherd of Hermas, described above)
- Ignatius of Antioch
- Polycarp of Smyrna

Later it became customary to add the anonymous Epistle to Diognetus and the Didache to the writings of the Apostolic Fathers. Scholars have concluded that these "apostolic fathers" had various accesses to writings that came to be part of the New Testament canon:

- Barnabas
    - Perhaps Matthew, 1 and 2 Timothy
- Clement of Rome
    - Romans, Galatians, Philippians, Ephesians, Hebrews
    - Perhaps Acts, James, 1 Peter
- Hermas
    - John, at least one of the Synoptic gospels, Ephesians, James
- Ignatius of Antioch
    - 1 Corinthians, Ephesians, Romans, Galatians, Philippians, Colossians, 1 Thessalonians, Matthew, John
    - Perhaps Hebrews, 1 Peter, Luke
- Polycarp of Smyrna
    - Romans, 1 Corinthians, Galatians, Ephesians, Philippians, 2 Thessalonians, 1 Timothy, 2 Timothy, Hebrews, 1 John, 1 Peter, Matthew, Luke

It should be noted that for all of these authors, "Scripture" was what we now know as the Old Testament. For early Christians, as for the Jews, the Bible consisted of the Old Testament and some Jewish apocryphal literature. For early Christians, however, along with the Hebrew Bible came the words of Jesus, in both written and oral form. The words of Jesus had supreme authority. Although the written gospels and Paul's letters had authority, there is no suggestion that these writings were regarded as "Scripture" by the apostolic fathers.

Chapter 5

After the New Testament

Timeline of Important Events

313 C.E.	Edict of Milan
325	Council of Nicaea
330	Constantinople made eastern capital
382	Jerome begins Vulgate translation
1054	Great Schism between Eastern (Greek) and Western (Latin) Churches
1095–1099	First Crusade
1202–1204	Fourth Crusade, sacking of Constantinople
1330–1384	John Wycliffe
1398–1468	Johannes Gutenberg
1455	Gutenberg prints the Vulgate Bible
1483–1546	Martin Luther
1494–1536	William Tyndale
1517	Luther's 95 Theses
1522–1534	Luther's German translation of the Bible
1611	King James (Authorized) Version of the Bible

The Roman Period
(200 to 313 C.E.)

The third century of the Common Era saw a continued slow growth of Christianity throughout the Roman Empire. Earlier on Christianity was seen as a sect within Judaism, but it later became seen as an independent religion. The movement probably started out as a group of several dozen lower-class peasants who were followers of Jesus and continued to believe in him after his death. Jesus was thoroughly Jewish: he was a Jewish prophet to the Jewish people. There was no evidence of an intention by Jesus to start a new religion. His teachings were drawn from the Hebrew Scriptures, and he followed Jewish customs including keeping the Sabbath and observing Jewish festivals. Early on the Roman authorities did not differentiate between Christian Jews and non-Christian Jews. However, the Emperor Nero did make a differentiation when he was looking for a scapegoat for a fire in Rome (which he apparently set himself). He blamed the Christians, not the Jews. A further separation between Jews and Christians happened a short time later during the uprising against the Romans that resulted in the destruction of the temple in 70 C.E. It appears Christian Jews did not participate in this uprising.

The apostles, particularly Paul of Tarsus, spread the gospel ("good news") throughout urban centers of the empire. Paul set up Christian churches in Cilicia, Asia Minor, Macedonia and Achaia (modern Turkey and Greece). At the end of the second-century Christians made up 2–3% of the population of the empire. At the end of the third century Christians made up about 5% of the Roman population. The Roman emperor, Constantine, converted to Christianity in 313 C.E., and then Christianity really took off. At the end of the fourth century, nearly half of the empire called itself Christian. The emperor Theodosius I (374–395) made it the official state religion at the end of the fourth century and outlawed pagan religious practices.

Christianity was never declared illegal by any Roman emperor until the middle of the third century. Up until then Christianity and all religions were tolerated. The problem for the Romans was not that Jews and Christians worshipped Yahweh and/or Jesus, but it was that they refused to worship the Roman gods or the emperor (an act of treason). It was believed that by making sacrifices to the various Roman gods, calamities were avoided. By not worshiping the Roman gods (a public, civic responsibility), Christians and Jews became scapegoats for any misfortunes that arose, e.g., droughts. The next emperor (after Nero) to be involved with persecutions of the Christians was Trajan (c. 112 C.E.). Now Christians could be persecuted simply because they acknowledged being Christian. However, if they recanted, they would be forgiven.

It was not until the middle of the third century that there was an empire-wide attempt to eliminate Christianity. Decius (249 C.E.) led a persecution, but it only lasted two years: Decius died in 251. The most significant persecution, known as the "Great Persecution" was led by Diocletian, and this lasted several years until Constantine became emperor (303–313). Christian churches and writings were destroyed, and Christian worship was forbidden. All of this changed in 313 when Constantine converted to Christianity, and he and Licinius met in Milan and jointly issued an edict, now known as the "Edict of Milan" which granted religious freedom not only to Christians but to all religions.

Some Christians were killed for their religious beliefs and were venerated by other Christians for being martyrs. Tertullian, the important second-century church father, said "the blood of martyrs is the seed of the Church." There is evidence that some early Christians actively sought out martyrdom, feeling that they would be rewarded in the afterlife. We see similar behavior today by Muslim extremists who commit suicide bombings for which they feel they'll be rewarded in heaven. One significant difference, however, is that the Christian martyrs did not commit violence to others.

There was tremendous diversity in beliefs amongst the various groups of people who called themselves Christians during the first couple centuries of the Common Era. Over the centuries since, people mistakenly believed that Christianity started off with a pure set of beliefs, the teachings of Jesus which were disseminated by his disciples and then by other generations of church leaders. It was believed that only over time did "heresies" or false teachings infiltrate the churches. This was the view taught by Eusebius (260–340). Actually early Christian beliefs were extremely diverse. There is great diversity even within the New Testament canon. The German scholar, Walter Bauer (1877–1960) and other scholars found that in the earliest Christian centers (Syria, Egypt, Asia Minor, Rome) "heretical" forms of Christianity were in evidence even before what is now known as "orthodox" forms. It was only over centuries that this "orthodox" or "proto-orthodox" view won out. The views of the Roman church eventually won out over a wide variety of other "Christianities." Three early groups of Christians whose beliefs did not win out were the **Ebionites**, the **Marcionites**, and the **gnostics**.

The Ebionites were a group of Jewish Christians who strictly followed Jewish laws, e.g., circumcision, kosher food, Sabbath observance). They believed that Jesus was the most righteous man to have ever lived, and because of this was "adopted" by God to be his son. It became his mission, as God's son, to die for the sins of mankind. It was no longer necessary to make sacrifices of animals after this. Jesus was rewarded by being raised from the dead. They stressed that Jesus was the *Jewish* messiah, and that any Gentiles who wanted to be right with God needed to become Jewish and observe all of the Jewish laws. They believed that Jesus was fully human and not divine. Joseph and Mary were his parents. These groups of Christians were not followers of Paul. It is thought by scholars that they used as Scripture a gospel very similar to the Gospel of Matthew and another gospel known as the Gospel of the Ebionites. The group was associated with James, the brother of Jesus.

The Marcionites were followers of the second-century theologian, Marcion. Their beliefs were diametrically opposed to those of the Ebionites: they rejected Judaism, saw Jesus as fully divine and not really human, were followers of the Apostle Paul, and were quite hostile to the Old Testament god, Yahweh. Marcion established churches in Asia Minor, where his churches thrived for centuries. Marcion saw the Old Testament god and the god of Jesus as being radically different, and so he believed there were two gods: the inferior, wrathful god of the Hebrew Scriptures who created the world, and the superior God of love and mercy who sent Jesus, who came to save the people of the world from the wrathful Old Testament god. Marcion was very aware of the contradictions between the teachings of Jesus (e.g., love your enemies) and directives of Yahweh, e.g., telling Joshua to have every man, woman, child, and animal killed in the land of Canaan. Marcion was the first to devise a canon of Scripture. It contained ten of Paul's letters (not 1 and 2 Timothy or Titus) and a gospel similar to Luke. The Old Testament was excluded. So to contrast the Ebionites and the Marcionites:

Ebionites	**Marcionites**
Monotheistic (one god)	Ditheist (two gods)
Embraced Jewish law	Rejected Jewish law
Jesus was human, not divine	Jesus was divine, not human
Perceived Paul as heretical	Revered Paul
Used a gospel similar to Matthew	Used a gospel similar to Luke

Another group of early Christians were known as gnostics. The term *gnosis* refers to knowledge. Gnostics believed that salvation came from having a secret self-knowledge, that is to say, knowledge of who we are, where we come from, and knowledge about the physical and spiritual worlds. They believed this material world was a world of imprisonment. The goal is for our divinity (spirit) to escape the evil, material, physical world of matter. In 1945 gnostic documents were uncovered in Egypt near the village of Nag Hammadi. These documents are now known as the Nag Hammadi library. This was a tremendous archeological discovery that has given us much more information about the gnostic Christians. The writings themselves were produced in the late fourth century but were believed to have been originally written in the second century or earlier. The writings contain 52 treatises and included several gospels and apocalypses.

Conversion of Constantine

The year 313 C.E. was a tremendous turning point in the history of Christianity. The Roman Emperor Constantine converted to Christianity. The persecution of Christians ceased. In 380 Emperor Theodosius I made Christianity the official state religion and ended state support for paganism and made paganism illegal. By the end of the fourth century half of the Roman Empire had become Christian. The persecuted became the persecutors. Christian individuals began vandalizing ancient pagan temples and monuments. The Roman government imposed new laws against participation in pagan sacrifices and the worship of idols. Temples were shut down. Violators could be given the death penalty. With the victory of Christianity also came anti-Jewish feelings. Judaism was seen as another false religion, and they became another persecuted minority in the Roman Empire.

A number of cities became centers of theological thought: Alexandria (in modern day Egypt), Antioch (in modern day Turkey), Rome, Constantinople, and Jerusalem (where the religion began). Rome, as the capital of the empire, had great clout, especially since it was the largest church in Christendom. A theology—labeled "proto-orthodoxy" by recent scholars—was espoused by the Roman church; it eventually won out over other Christian theologies.

Ecumenical Councils

Christianity as a religion was quite unique in stressing the importance of believing the right things. Religions of that day, including paganism, stressed the importance of rituals, not belief. Even Judaism stressed more keeping laws and observing festivals rather than believing a particular way. For example, there was no consensus among the Jews in regards to there being an afterlife. Pharisees believed in it generally, and Sadducees did not.

Many people believe that Constantine converted to Christianity at least partly because of seeing it as a vehicle for uniting the empire. Despite the victory of the proto-orthodox theology, there continued to be significant doctrinal differences in the Christian churches that Constantine feared was interfering with the unity of the empire. In particular he wanted to resolve what was known as the "Arian controversy" (named after Arius who maintained that Jesus was supreme among God's creatures but was not fully divine). He therefore convened and financed a Christian council in 325 C.E. that represented all of Christendom. It met in the city of Nicaea. The council decided against Arius and said that Jesus was "of one substance" with God and that Jesus was both human and divine. Also decided at this council was the date that Easter would be celebrated, and probably most importantly the creation of a creed, known as the "Nicene Creed." This is a translation of the original:

Nicene Creed of 325:

We believe in one God,
the Father almighty,
maker of all things visible and invisible;
And in one Lord, Jesus Christ,
the Son of God,
begotten from the Father, only-begotten,
that is, from the substance of the Father,
God from God,
light from light,
true God from true God,
begotten not made,
of one substance with the Father,
through Whom all things came into being,
things in heaven and things on earth,
Who because of us men and because of our salvation came down,
and became incarnate
and became man,
and suffered,
and rose again on the third day,
and ascended to the heavens,
and will come to judge the living and dead,
And in the Holy Spirit.
But as for those who say, There was when He was not,
and, Before being born He was not,
and that He came into existence out of nothing,
or who assert that the Son of God is of a different hypostasis or
substance,
or created,
or is subject to alteration or change

—these the Catholic and apostolic Church anathematizes.

Although the beliefs and concepts of this creed should not seem unusual to Christians today, they were issues that were highly debated and were very controversial at that time. Remember that the Ebionites saw Jesus as fully human and not divine, and the Marcionites saw Jesus as fully divine and not human. Jesus Christ's essence continued to be a topic of debate, even after the Council of Nicaea. The controversies primarily resolved around the issue of a "**Trinity**." It must be remembered that the delegates to the Council of Nicaea could not consult their New Testaments to answer these questions; there was no New Testament canon at this time. Even if they did have a copy of our New Testament, there is no exposition of this concept by Jesus, Paul, or any writer in the New Testament. The only passage in the New Testament that mentions a trinity is 1 John 5:7–8: "There are three that testify: the Spirit and the water and the blood, and these three agree."

The King James Version of these two verses is "For there are three that bear record in heaven, the Father, the Word, and the Holy Ghost: and these three are one. And there are three that bear witness in earth, the Spirit, and the water, and the blood: and these three agree in one."

These verses were believed to have been expanded by a scribe at a much later date to support a Trinitarian doctrine. It is not found in *any* Greek manuscript until the 11th century. Probably the first to elaborate a doctrine of God as being "Three in One" was the Christian apologist Athenagoras in the second century.

What I think is particularly striking about the Nicene Creed (and another famous creed, the Apostle's Creed) is that there is no mention at all about Jesus' actual teachings. Jesus' actual life and ministry are apparently found to be completely irrelevant in these creeds. What Jesus himself found important—his life work is never mentioned!

There was a total of seven ecumenical councils that met over the years, and the main topic of debate continued to be Jesus' nature, i.e., how human and how divine.

- 381 C.E. Second Ecumenical Council (The First Council of Constantinople)
    - o Dealt with Apollinarism (that Jesus had a human body but a divine mind). It was deemed heresy
    - o This council also produced a revision of the Nicene Creed.
- 431 C.E. Third Ecumenical Council (The Council of Ephesus)
    - o Dealt with Nestorianism (that there is a disunion between the human and divine natures of Jesus). It was deemed heresy.
- 451 C.E. Fourth Ecumenical Council (The Council of Chalcedon)
    - o Dealt with Monophysitism (belief that after the union of the divine and human in Jesus' incarnation, Jesus then had a single nature which was either divine or a synthesis of the divine and human).
- 553 C.E. Fifth Ecumenical Council (The Second Council of Constantinople)
    - o Dealt with Nestorianism again.
- 681 C.E. Sixth Ecumenical Council (The Third Council of Constantinople)

- o Dealth with Monothelitism (the view that Jesus has two natures but only one will). It was deemed heresy.
- 787 C.E. Seventh Ecumenical Council (The Second Council of Nicaea)
    - o This council did not deal with Trinitarian issues. It restored the veneration of icons.

It took centuries for the doctrine of the Trinity to be developed. The doctrine of the Trinity presents a problem: if Jesus is God, how can one still say that there is only one God and still be a monotheist. There were many ideas about the solution to this problem, and the problem required great creativity in thinking. Some early theologians (e.g., Sabellius, Praxeas) taught that God the Father, Jesus the son, and the Holy Spirit were different aspects of the one God rather than three coeternal persons. This was deemed heresy. Tertullian particularly objected to the idea that God the Father could have suffered on the cross.

One of the greatest early Christian theologians, Origen of Alexandria, postulated that Jesus began just like all human beings: a preexistent soul created to contemplate God. But Jesus, unlike the rest of us, accomplished this to such an extent that he actually became "one" with God. This too was condemned as heresy because it subordinated Jesus to God the father.

Theologian Tertullian's formulation came to be accepted as the right way of thinking about this. Tertullian said that God is three in degree, but not condition. God is three in form but not in substance. God is three in aspect but not in power.

Church Offices

Initially Christian church communities were "charismatic," i.e., run by community members utilizing "gifts of the spirit." It was believed that church communities would be short lived, as Christ was expected to return soon to bring a new kingdom to earth. Eventually a more hierarchical structure was imposed on the churches. Ignatius insisted that a bishop be the overseer of each church, and that he be assisted by presbyters and deacons who served under him. Congregants were expected to be obedient to these bishops. The largest Christian church was the Church of Rome, and the bishop of Rome came to be seen—at least in the West—as the head of the church at large. The bishop of Rome would come to be known as the pope, the leader over the entire church. Church offices were important for individual's understanding of the Bible. Because individuals did not have access to scripture (and probably couldn't read anyways), they relied on priests and bishops to teach them what to believe.

Canonization

In the early Christian churches, various writings were used by various churches as "Scripture." Eventually both Christians and Jews sought to establish a "canon," that is, a fixed set of writings that were not only authoritative (as Scripture was thought to be) but also correct in its teachings and of special significance. Thus the term "canon" is more restrictive than "Scripture." At the end of the second century, Christians began to consider what was in the "Old Testament" canon, and this continued to be debated into the fifth century. It was not until the fourth century that lists of

Christian writings were formulated that were considered canonical. Thus during the first four centuries of Christianity there were Scriptures, but no canon. However, in the earliest centuries Christianity did not center on Scriptures; it centered on Jesus Christ, most known by oral traditions of his words and deeds. There is no evidence of anything being written about him until decades after his death, and these writings were likely not by eyewitnesses.

As mentioned previously, probably the first canonical list was that of Marcion (100–160 C.E.). It contained ten of Paul's letters (not including 1 and 2 Timothy or Titus) and a gospel similar to Luke. The Old Testament was excluded. It should be remembered that the Marcionites were considered heretical by the proto-orthodox.

An ironic fact is that many people today venerate the Bible as the one and only word of God. It is the Bible that teaches us the right way to think about God and Jesus. Yet decisions were made about what Scriptures should be put into the Bible based on what those individuals thought was the right way of thinking. It also should be remembered that all of the writers whose compositions made it into the canon were not consciously writing "Scripture" that they expected to be put into an authoritative canon. The gospel writers put to paper the oral stories they heard about Jesus' acts and words. Much of the New Testament canon is letters written to particular church communities to address particular problems, e.g., the letters of Paul, the major contributor to the New Testament. Interestingly, although Paul's collected letters were available by the early second century, they were mostly used by Marcion and the gnostics. They gradually attained broader use throughout the Christian world over the second century and attained scriptural standing.

The fourth and fifth centuries were the period of canon formation. One of the earliest canonical lists was the **"Muratorian Canon,"** likely dated to the fourth century but possibly as early as the late second century. It listed:

- Matthew, Mark, Luke, and John
- Acts
- Thirteen letters attributed to Paul
- Jude
- First and Second John
- The Wisdom of Solomon (curious in that it is a writing of the intertestamental period)
- Revelation
- Apocalypse of Peter

Thus the Muratorian Canon included two writings that *did not* eventually make it into the New Testament canon (The Wisdom of Solomon and the Apocalypse of Peter) and did not include five writings that *did* make it into the canon (Hebrews, James, 1 and 2 Peter, 3 John).

In the fourth and fifth centuries the gospels of Matthew, Mark, Luke, and John were accepted out of all the gospels that had been written as the primary, authoritative gospels. The early church father, **Irenaeus** (130–200 C.E.), taught that the gospel which was originally preached orally was eventually put to writing. He conceptualized a single gospel in four forms (the four gospels) and said there could only be four gospels:

> "It is not possible that the Gospels can be either more or fewer in number than they are, since there are four directions of the world in which we are, and

four principal winds...The four living creatures (referenced in Revelation 4) symbolize the four Gospels. . . and there were four principal covenants made with humanity, through Noah, Abraham, Moses, and Christ. "

Cyprian of Carthage in the third century said that the Gospels are four in number like the rivers of paradise in Genesis. So both Irenaeus and Cyprian said there should be only four gospels in the New Testament canon not because there weren't other gospels that were inspired, but for other reasons to restrict the number to four.

Eusebius writing in the fourth century lists writings that he believes are considered accepted without qualification, writings that are disputed and writings that are considered heretical:

Accepted	**Disputed**	**Heretical**
Matthew	James	Gospel of Peter
Mark	Jude	Gospel of Thomas
Luke	2 Peter	Gospel of Matthias
John	2-3 John	Acts of Andrew
Acts	Acts of Paul	Acts of John
13 letters of Paul	Shepherd of Hermas	
Hebrews	Apocalypse of Peter	
1 John	Epistle of Barnabas	
1 Peter	the Didache	
	Revelation	

About 332 C.E. Emperor Constantine directed Eusebius to have 50 copies of sacred Scripture to be made by accomplished scribes. Amazingly, we have nothing from Eusebius telling us which writings he included in these 50

Bibles and in which sequence. It is almost certain that Eusebius's choice had tremendous influence on future editions of a canon. This is probably the first instance in which we can speak of the Bible as a "book."

The **Cheltenham Canon** is a mid-fourth century list from North Africa. It lists the four gospels, 13 letters of Paul, Acts, Revelation, 1-3 John, and 1-2 Peter. It leaves out James, Jude, and Hebrews.

The list of **Athanasius** (300–375 C.E.) appears to be the first that lists the exact 27 books that are in our current New Testament.

Although the four gospels, Acts, the letters of Paul, 1 Peter, and 1 John were almost universally accepted in the fourth and fifth centuries, other writings were more controversial. Particularly disputed was the Book of Revelation which was accepted in the West but generally rejected in the East. Ecclesiastical councils took up the question of canonicity in the fourth and fifth centuries. The **Council of Laodicea** (363) named 26 books as canonical, omitting Revelation. The **Council of Hippo** (393) and the **Council of Carthage** (397) named our current 27 books.

In order to be considered for canonicity, writings needed to be in agreement with what the church took to be apostolic teaching, needed to be written during the earliest times, and needed to conform to what the church felt was proper teaching. So true belief does not come from Scripture, it precedes it. There was not a conception that Scripture was the sole source of authoritative teaching. There was no claim in the ancient church that canonical documents were uniquely or exclusively inspired.

Writing and Copying Manuscripts

We do not have original copies of any of the writings that are found in either the Old or the New Testaments. The reason the Dead Sea Scrolls were such an important find was that they provided Hebrew texts that were copied more than a thousand years earlier than any Hebrew texts we previously had. Some manuscripts date to the third century B.C.E. The scrolls were written in Hebrew, Aramaic, and Greek.

It is important for biblical scholars to find the earliest possible manuscripts to discover the message of the original authors. There were no printing presses, so each manuscript was made by hand by a scribe who copied another manuscript. In the copying process we know that mistakes were made; some intentional and some unintentional. If you can imagine yourself copying a Bible word-for-word by hand, it is easy to imagine how unintentional mistakes would occur. It is particularly easy to understand if one realizes that early Greek used no punctuation, had no separation between sentences and paragraphs, used no spaces to separate words, and made no distinction between lowercase and uppercase letters.

Most of the manuscripts that we have of the New Testament came from the Middle Ages, over a thousand years after the originals. Copies had been made from copies, from copies, from copies, etc. If we compare these various manuscripts, we find hundreds of thousands of differences. New Testament scholar Bart Ehrman puts it this way: "there are more differences in our manuscripts than there are words in the New Testament." However, most of these discrepancies are unimportant, for example spelling errors. There are some important discrepancies as well though, and these are likely due to intentional errors.

Intentional mistakes would occur by scribes who thought they were reading mistakes and then "correcting" them, thereby making mistakes. Ehrman in his book, *The Orthodox Corruption of Scripture (2011)*, maintains that proto-orthodox scribes occasionally modified texts of Scripture to make it more align with the theological viewpoints of the proto-orthodox, the "winning" theology of the time. As I mentioned previously, 1 John 5:7–8 does not appear in Greek versions of the New Testament until the 11th century. It had evidently been added by a scribe who felt there needed to be justification for a Trinitarian doctrine. The Gospel of Mark originally ended with several women finding Jesus' tomb empty. They fled and said nothing to anyone because they were afraid. Verses 9–20 of Mark 16 were added later. These verses were not found in our earliest manuscripts of Mark, and the writing style and vocabulary is not consistent with the rest of the gospel.

Originally our New Testament writings (or Old Testament) did not have chapters or numbered verses. Chapter division may have started as early as the fourth century, but today's chapter divisions go back to the beginning of the 13th century. Verse divisions did not come along until the 16th century.

Early Translations of the Bible

The "Old Testament" was written in Hebrew, and the "New Testament" was written in Greek. From early times the Bible got translated into other languages. Early translations were into Syriac for the Syriac Christians and Coptic for the Egyptian Christians. Of particular importance was the translation of the Bible into Latin, the language of the Western church centered in Rome (Greek continued to be the language of the Eastern Church centered in Constantinople). Pope Damascus (304–384) assigned the great Christian scholar, Jerome, to develop a dependable text of the Bible into Latin, which he did using the Hebrew Scripture as his source for the Old Testament rather than the Septuagint (LXX). Jerome's Bible included all of the Hebrew canonical books, Tobit and Judith from LXX, the Four Gospels, Acts, Letters, and Revelation. The Vulgate became *the* biblical source for the Western Church. Other early translations of Scripture were into Armenian, Georgian, Ethiopian, and Gothic.

Medieval Period
(Fifth to 15th Centuries)

During this time period **monasteries** developed. These were religious communities devoted to worship, Christian work, and religious study. In an illiterate world, they were havens of literacy and learning. They were centers for the production of Bibles. Monks spent much of their lives immersed in the Bible. A main occupation in the monasteries was copying and preserving manuscripts. I mentioned previously that in the process of copying manuscripts there were often inadvertent errors. This appears to be much more the case in the earlier years of Christianity when the individuals doing the copying were not "professionals." The monks appeared to do a very good job in accurately copying biblical manuscripts. Unfortunately, they likely unknowingly copied earlier mistakes from previous copyists.

In the Medieval Period most individuals were illiterate, and, regardless, there was not yet the invention of the printing press and books were very rare. Therefore, the Bible was not experienced by people by reading a book. Rather Scripture was usually a communal experience in which Scripture was transmitted orally. At mass, Scripture was read from a lectionary and then elaborated on in a homily. The belief developed that God was the author of all Scripture and that the Bible spoke in a unified and harmonious fashion. The New Testament was seen as a continuation of the Old Testament. The Bible was not examined in a critical manner because people did not have access to the written word to do this. The clergy told the parishioners what to believe. This was the period in which the great gothic cathedrals were built. These magnificent structures which took centuries to build were another source in which people could experience God. The stained glass windows in these edifices told the biblical stories, and rituals helped teach the Christian religion.

Islam

It was during this Medieval Period that **Islam** developed. This is an important event for the history of the Bible for several reasons. Tradition has it that **Muhammad** was born in 570 C.E., although the exact date really is not known. He grew up an orphan in Mecca, which is in present day Saudi

Arabia. It is believed that he had contact with Christians, Zoroastrians, Jews, and Hanifism (a monotheistic religious movement that arose in pre-Islamic Arabia). Muhammad began to receive direct revelations from God. Muslims believe there have been revelations from God to prophets in many religions, and these prophets have included Adam, Moses, David, and Jesus. Muhammad's revelations were considered the most important and are the only ones believed to be a direct revelation from God. So in Islam the Qur'an is believed to be a new revelation from God, a "new testament" if you will. Islam is also important in that much of the Eastern Christian church converted to Islam. This included the important Christian centers of Egypt, Syria, and Jerusalem.

The Renaissance
(14ᵗʰ to 17ᵗʰ Centuries)

The Renaissance, which originated in Italy, represents a change in worldview. This is partly the result of Columbus's discovery of the New World in 1492, Copernicus's (1473–1543) theory that the earth revolved around the sun (and that the earth was not the center of the solar system), a new willingness to question old paradigms, and the development of more advanced scientific methodology resulting in scientific advancements. Perhaps the most important invention was the printing press. **Johannes Gutenberg** (1398–1468) developed a new type of printing press which brought printing to Europe. Now for the first time books could be mass produced, and now for the first time books became available to the general public. Gutenberg published a two-volume version of the Vulgate in 1455. Now people could read the Bible rather than just hear portions recited at mass.

The Reformation

This period is also important for the **Protestant Reformation**. In 1517 a German priest named **Martin Luther** posted 95 theses on the door of All Saints Church in Wittenberg. In these theses he particularly objected to the sale of indulgences (people could atone for sins by giving money to the church). Thanks to the printing press the theses were printed and widely distributed. Among other things, Luther taught that the Bible was the only source of divinely revealed knowledge about God. He believed in the principles of *sola fide* (by faith alone) and *sola scriptura* (Scripture alone). He believed it was only by faith in Jesus Christ that people were saved—not in good works. He believed the Bible was the supreme authority on God and doctrine. These principles were paramount to all of the Protestant reformers.

The original creeds of the Christian church, the Apostles Creed and the Nicene Creed, do not mention the Bible at all. Now with the Reformation new creeds were developed that declare the supremacy of the Bible:

- **The Augsburg Confession** (1530) stresses that all Christian teachings should be "grounded clearly on the Holy Scriptures."
- **Ten Conclusions of Berne** (1528) says "The church of Christ makes no laws or commandments apart from the word of God."
- **Second Helvetic Confession** (1566). "We believe and confess the canonical Scriptures of the holy

prophets and apostles of both testaments to be the true word of God, and to have sufficient authority of themselves, not of men."
- **Westminster Confession** (1646). "The infallible rule of interpretation of Scripture is the Scripture itself."
- The sixth of the **Thirty-Nine Articles** (1563) says that nothing should be believed except what can be based in Scripture.

Another important contribution of Martin Luther was the translation of the Bible into German. Luther considered four of the books of the New Testament to be inferior to the others: Hebrews, James (because it declared that faith without works is dead), Jude, and Revelation. Luther also interpreted the Bible very literally compared to many predecessors. Luther's main criteria for a biblical book's authority was whether it agreed with his thoughts theologically. Whatever does not teach Christ is not apostolic, even though St. Peter or St. Paul does the teaching. Again, whatever preaches Christ would be apostolic, even if Judas, Annas, Pilate, and Herod were doing it." So in other words, it is not so important who the writer was or when it was written; what matters is whether it says the right things (according to Luther). Luther's translation of the New Testament was completed in 1522, and the Old Testament in 1534.

John Wycliffe, an Oxford theologian, spearheaded an effort to translate the Bible into English even earlier. He believed that the Bible was the sole criterion for Christian doctrine and was the word of God addressed to each individual. So he felt a strong need for each individual to be able to read it for themselves. It is unlikely that Wycliffe himself was involved in the translation of the Latin Vulgate Bible into English, but he was the impetus. The Bibles were handwritten, as printing had not yet been invented. The first version was produced in 1382. A second version appeared in 1388. John Wycliffe was an outspoken critic of the Catholic Church, and as a result he was condemned posthumously by the Council of Constance in 1415. Wycliffe Bibles were burned. Wycliffe's body was exhumed and burned and his ashes cast into a river.

William Tyndale (1492–1536) was a skilled linguist (fluent in eight languages) who studied at Oxford and then Cambridge. He decided to translate the Bible into English. He worked from the Hebrew and Greek rather than the Latin Vulgate. The first edition of the New Testament was printed in 1526, the Pentateuch and Psalms in 1530, and Jonah in 1531. Job through 2 Chronicles was in the process of being translated at the time of Tyndale's death. Because the 1408 Constitutions of Oxford strictly forbade the translation of the Bible into native tongues, Tyndale was strangled while tied to a stake. His dead body was then burned. His last words were "Lord, open the king of England's eyes." His prayer was answered; in 1537 Henry VIII allowed the English Bible to be distributed. Although Tyndale and others felt that individuals should be able to read the Bible on their own, others in the church felt the teachings of the Bible were too obscure for uneducated people to elucidate and that it therefore required theologically educated individuals (priests) to explain the teachings of the Bible.

The first complete printed English Bible was published by **Miles Coverdale** (1488–1568). Thomas Matthew, the pseudonym of John Rogers, published a version of the Bible in 1537 (known as Matthew's Bible) before dying as a martyr. "The Great Bible" was published by Thomas Cromwell in 1539. It got its name due to its size. It was the first "authorized" English Bible.

Different Bibles

After the Reformation, when talking about the Bible there really were four different versions: the Jewish Bible, the Protestant Bible, the Catholic Bible, and the Eastern Orthodox Bible. The compositions of each of these were different and are shown below. It should be noted that the chronologies of these books vary within the different biblical canons. The table below does not show the correct order of books necessarily within a canon.

Hebrew Bible	Protestant Bible	Catholic Bible	Orthodox Bible
Genesis	Genesis	Genesis	Genesis
Exodus	Exodus	Exodus	Exodus
Leviticus	Leviticus	Leviticus	Leviticus
Numbers	Numbers	Numbers	Numbers
Deuteronomy	Deuteronomy	Deuteronomy	Deuteronomy
Joshua	Joshua	Joshua	Joshua
Judges	Judges	Judges	Judges
1 and 2 Samuel	1 and 2 Samuel	1 and 2 Samuel	1 and 2 Samuel
1 and 2 Kings	1 and 2 Kings	1 and 2 Kings	1 and 2 Kings
Isaiah	Isaiah	Isaiah	Isaiah
Jeremiah	Jeremiah	Jeremiah	Jeremiah
Ezekiel	Ezekiel	Ezekiel	Ezekiel
Hosea	Hosea	Hosea	Hosea
Joel	Joel	Joel	Joel
Amos	Amos	Amos	Amos
Obadiah	Obadiah	Obadiah	Obadiah
Jonah	Jonah	Jonah	Jonah
Micah	Micah	Micah	Micah
Nahum	Nahum	Nahum	Nahum
Habakkuk	Habakkuk	Habakkuk	Habakkuk
Zephaniah	Zephaniah	Zephaniah	Zephaniah
Haggai	Haggai	Haggai	Haggai
Zechariah	Zechariah	Zechariah	Zechariah
Malachi	Malachi	Malachi	Malachi
Psalms	Psalms	Psalms	Psalms
Proverbs	Proverbs	Proverbs	Proverbs

Job	Job	Job	Job
Song of Solomon	Song of Solomon	Song of Solomon	Song of Solomon
Ruth	Ruth	Ruth	Ruth
Lamentations	Lamentations	Lamentations	Lamentations
Ecclesiastes	Ecclesiastes	Ecclesiastes	Ecclesiastes
Esther	Esther	Esther	Esther
Daniel	Daniel	Daniel	Daniel
Ezra-Nehemiah	Ezra-Nehemiah	Ezra-Nehemiah	Ezra-Nehemiah
1 and 2 Chronicles	1 and 2 Chronicles	1 and 2 Chronicles	1 and 2 Chronicles
		Tobit	Tobit
		Judith	Judith
		1 Maccabees	1 Maccabees
		2 Maccabees	2 Maccabees
			3 Maccabees
			4 Maccabees
			1 and 2 Esdras
		Wisdom of Solomon	Wisdom of Solomon
		Sirach	Sirach
		Baruch	Baruch
			Letter of Jeremiah
	Matthew	Matthew	Matthew
	Mark	Mark	Mark
	Luke	Luke	Luke
	John	John	John
	Acts of the Apostles	Acts of the Apostles	Acts of the Apostles
	Romans	Romans	Romans
	1 and 2 Corinthians	1 and 2 Corinthians	1 and 2 Corinthians
	Galatians	Galatians	Galatians
	Ephesians	Ephesians	Ephesians
	Philippians	Philippians	Philippians
	Colossians	Colossians	Colossians
	1 and 2 Thessalonians	1 and 2 Thessalonians	1 and 2 Thessalonians
	1 and 2 Timothy	1 and 2 Timothy	1 and 2 Timothy
	Titus	Titus	Titus
	Philemon	Philemon	Philemon
	Hebrews	Hebrews	Hebrews
	James	James	James
	1 and 2 Peter	1 and 2 Peter	1 and 2 Peter
	1, 2, and 3 John	1, 2, and 3 John	1, 2, and 3 John
	Jude	Jude	Jude
	Revelation	Revelation	Revelation

King James Bible

In 1604 King James of England endorsed the idea of a new "authorized" English version of the Bible, as he was dissatisfied with all of the English versions at that time. The most common Bible at that time was the **Geneva Bible**, which King James was very dissatisfied with. Approximately 50 "learned" men comprised a translation committee. In 1611 the **King James Bible** was first published. This is the most well-known English Bible of all time. The most well-known passages from the Bible we generally know are in the language of the King James Version. For example:

- John 1:3 "All things were made by him; and without him was not anything made that was made."
- Rom. 12:2 "And be not conformed to this world: but be ye transformed by the renewing of your mind, that ye may prove what is that good, and acceptable, and perfect, will of God."
- Rev. 21:4 "And God shall wipe away all tears from their eyes; and there shall be no more death, neither sorrow, nor crying, neither shall there be any more pain: for the former things are passed away."
- Prov. 22:6 "Train up a child in the way he should go: and when he is old, he will not depart from it."
- Eccles. 3:1 "To everything there is a season, and a time to every purpose under the heaven: A time to be born, and a time to die; a time to plant, and a time to pluck up that which is planted."
- Ps. 118:24 "This is the day which the Lord hath made; we will rejoice and be glad in it."

- Matt. 7:7 "Ask, and it shall be given you; seek, and ye shall find; knock, and it shall be opened unto you."
- Matt. 11:28 "Come unto me, all ye that labour and are heavy laden, and I will give you rest."
- Isa. 9:6 "For unto us a child is born, unto us a son is given: and the government shall be upon his shoulder: and his name shall be called Wonderful, Counsellor, The mighty God, The everlasting Father, The Prince of Peace."
- John 3:16 "For God so loved the world, that he gave his only begotten Son, that whosoever believeth in him should not perish, but have everlasting life."
- Matt. 22:37 "Jesus said unto him, Thou shalt love the Lord thy God with all thy heart, and with all thy soul, and with all thy mind."
- 1 Cor. 13:11 "When I was a child, I spake as a child, I understood as a child, I thought as a child: but when I became a man, I put away childish things."
- Deut. 6:5 "And thou shalt love the Lord thy God with all thine heart, and with all thy soul, and with all thy might."
- Ps. 51:10 "Create in me a clean heart, O God; and renew a right spirit within me."

And of course Psalm 23:

- The LORD *is* my shepherd; I shall not want. He maketh me to lie down in green pastures: he leadeth me beside the still waters. He restoreth my soul: he leadeth me in the paths of righteousness for his name's sake. Yea, though I walk through the valley of the shadow of death, I will fear no evil: for thou *art* with me; thy rod and thy staff they comfort me. Thou preparest a table before me in the presence of mine enemies: thou anointest my head with oil; my cup runneth over. Surely goodness and mercy shall follow me all the days of my life: and I will dwell in the house of the LORD for ever

Although now over 400 years old and thus with very antiquated language, it was very beautifully and poetically written. The King James Version is still in regular use, and some Christians maintain that it is still the best and preferred English version of the Bible.

Although the translators who comprised the King James Bible used the earliest Hebrew and Greek sources that were available to them at that time, earlier manuscripts have been uncovered since, most notably the Dead Sea Scrolls. Whereas the earliest available manuscripts were from the tenth century C.E., numerous manuscripts are now available from as early as the second century. Newer translations of the Bible have used these earliest sources, and so many scholars believe that these newer translations are superior to the KJV (i.e., closer to the original writer's words). I have chosen to use the New Revised Standard Version of the Bible for my biblical quotations in this book.

Book of Mormon

Another important event in the evolution of the Bible was the publication of the Book of Mormon in 1830. Mormons believe that a heavenly angel named Moroni visited Joseph Smith and gave him access to writings of God's prophets who lived on the American continent. The early prophet

Levi reportedly lived in Jerusalem around 600 B.C.E.; God commanded Levi to lead a small group of people to the American continent. They developed a civilization in America that Jesus visited after his death and resurrection. The Book of Mormon reportedly contains the teachings of Jesus Christ to the people of America. Social scientist Dr. Mark Koltko-Rivera in his book *The Rise of the Mormons: Latter-day Saint Growth in the 21st Century* describes how the Mormons grew from a tiny group in the 1830s to being the fourth-largest church in America in 2012. He predicts that by 2120 it will become the largest or second largest church in the United States and the second largest religious body in the world with two billion members.

Biblical Politics

Politics can play some role in biblical translations. Take the hot button issue of homosexuality, for example. Note how the Greek word *malakos* in 1 Cor. 6:9–10 has been translated differently in different versions of the Bible. In the Latin Vulgate it was translated to *molles*. In both Greek and Latin the words *malakos* and *molles* literally mean "soft." In the Tyndale and Coverdale Bibles of the 1500s the word was translated as "weaklings."

In the King James and Douay-Rheims versions the word was translated as "effeminate":

> Know ye not that the unrighteous shall not inherit the kingdom of God? Be not deceived: neither fornicators, nor idolaters, nor adulterers, nor effeminate, nor abusers of themselves with mankind, Nor thieves, nor covetous, nor drunkards, nor

revilers, nor extortioners, shall inherit the kingdom of God. (KJV, 1611)

Know you not that the unjust shall not possess the kingdom of God? Do not err: neither fornicators, nor idolaters, nor adulterers, Nor the effeminate, nor liers with mankind, nor thieves, nor covetous, nor drunkards, nor railers, nor extortioners, shall possess the kingdom of God. (Douay-Rheims American Edition, 1899)

New Testament scholar Dr. Dale Martin from Yale University has eloquently explained that the word *malakos* "can refer to many things: the softness of expensive clothes, the richness and delicacy of gourmet food, the gentleness of light winds and breezes. When used as a term of moral condemnation, the word still refers to something perceived as 'soft': laziness, degeneracy, decadence, lack of courage, or, to sum up all these vices in one ancient category, the feminine." In that culture, masculinity was a virtue and femininity was a shortcoming. Although to be sexually penetrated was *malakoi* (whether it be men or women), *malakoi* was a much broader concept.

When the Revised Standard Version (RSV) of the Bible appeared in 1952, it received criticism from some for not being conservative enough theologically (and politically). Subsequently other versions of the Bible were published by these more theologically conservative groups. Note in the two versions below how the meaning of malakos has changed significantly to "homosexuals" or "men who have sex with men."

> Or do you not know that the unrighteous will not inherit the kingdom of God? Do not be deceived; neither fornicators, nor idolaters, nor adulterers, nor effeminate, nor homosexuals, nor thieves, nor *the* covetous, nor drunkards, nor revilers, nor swindlers, will inherit the kingdom of God. (New American Standard Bible, 1971)

> Or do you not know that wrongdoers will not inherit the kingdom of God? Do not be deceived: Neither the sexually immoral nor idolaters nor adulterers nor men who have sex with men nor thieves nor the greedy nor drunkards nor slanderers nor swindlers will inherit the kingdom of God. (New American Standard Bible, 1978)

The Bible is the world's bestselling and most read book. At the end of 2005, the Bible had been translated into 2,043 of the world's 6,500 languages. It has been estimated that there have been around 300 English translations of the Bible. Despite this, the vast majority of the general population is uninformed about the history of the Bible. The information that I have presented in this book is taught in academic courses at universities throughout the country and also is taught in mainstream seminaries. Unfortunately, it is seldom taught in our churches. My hope is that this succinct book will help in educating Christians and others about the history of the Bible. For more detailed information about the topics I have talked about in this book please refer to the bibliography in this book.

Postface

I once believed that the Bible was written by God and came to mankind pretty much as we have it now. I now know that what we have as the Bible is actually writings by many people who wrote over several centuries. There are indeed many contradictions in the Bible; in fact, Steve Wells who wrote *The Skeptic's Annotated Bible* identified 462 contradictions. Of course, contradictions would not be unexpected if you realized that many people were writing about their own experiences with God. When you realize the Bible did not come directly from God verbatim, then one would realize that there would be conflicts with history and science, and Steve Wells identifies 428 of such conflicts. These writers were not historians or scientists. The great early theologian, Augustine, recognized this; in his work *The Literal Meaning of Genesis,* he cautions Christians to reevaluate their interpretations of Scripture based on science so as not to sound ignorant to non-Christians, which would dissuade non-Christians from taking the Christians seriously in more important matters.

In studying the Hebrew Scriptures (Old Testament), I found it very interesting to note how Judaism evolved over the centuries. We can get a very different perception of Judaism when we realize that all of the writings were not written simultaneously, and that instead we should look at the writings in their historical context. At the beginning of this book, I listed the books of the Hebrew Bible in their historical periods, i.e., during the divided kingdoms of Israel and Judah (when the earliest books of the Hebrew Scriptures were written), during the Babylonian Period, during the Persian Period, and during the Greek Period. One can see an evolution in the Hebrew religion. The religion started in a culture that was polytheistic; people believed that there were many gods. The Israelites and their ancestors were unique in being henotheists, which means that although they accepted the existence of many gods, they worshiped only one God, Yahweh. Of course the Israelites often strayed from this injunction; from time to time they would worship other gods, such as Baal. It was not until "Second Isaiah" (in the 500s B.C.E.) that we get a clear statement of monotheism, that there is in fact only one God in existence.

> I am the Lord, and there is no other; besides me there is no god. (Isa. 45:5)

The early followers of Yahweh, starting with Abraham, made burnt offerings and circumcised their males to show their devotion to Yahweh. That was all that was required. Later Moses gave detailed laws and rituals to the Israelite people so as to differentiate themselves from other local cultures. There was no book, no Bible, no prescription for how one should believe. The requirements were offerings, circumcision, and following the law. No mention is made of a book (the Torah) until the prophet Ezra (400s B.C.E.) returns from the Babylonian captivity to Palestine with "the book of the law of Moses" (Neh. 8:1). This is the first we hear of the beginnings of a "Bible." Shortly after this the Torah may have achieved canonical status. The full Hebrew Scripture as we know it today did not achieve canonical status until the second century of the Common Era.

The title of this book is *Evolution of the Bible*, and indeed it did take many centuries for the Bible to develop. The Torah (Genesis, Exodus, Leviticus, Numbers, and Deuteronomy) achieved canonical status as early as the fifth century B.C.E. The entire Hebrew Bible, however, did not take final shape until the second century of the Common Era. In Judaism, even at the time of Jesus, there was no emphasis on a correct way to believe. The Pharisees stressed keeping the Jewish law. The Sadducees stressed making temple sacrifices.

I do not believe the Hebrew Scriptures would be well known to the world outside the Jewish community if not for Jesus. The writings were written by Jews for Jews. However, because Christianity became the dominant religion of the world, Jesus' religion became our religion. Christianity was seen as a continuation and fulfillment of the Hebrew Scriptures. This is the new testament, the continuation of the old testament.

As far as the New Testament, many Scriptures were considered "inspired" and were used by various Christian communities in the first couple of centuries of the Common Era. The canon as we have it today (27 books) finally came together in the fourth century. A certain theological viewpoint, known as the proto-orthodox, won out amongst competing theologies. The Scriptures that were accepted into the New Testament canon were those writings that mostly conformed to that theology. However, there was not the belief at that time that the canon was the *only* source for knowledge of God and Jesus. The early creeds did not even mention the Bible. It was not until the Reformation that the idea of *sola scriptura* really took off and that the Bible, for all practical purposes, began to be worshiped.

In my studies I have learned that early Christianity was very diverse. There were many different beliefs about the nature of Jesus. There were many different Scriptures to reflect these varying beliefs. I've learned that there were many writings considered "Scripture" by various groups, many writings considered "inspired" by God, but that only a few of these made it into the Christian "canon." Whereas many Christians today think that the sole way to know what to believe about God is through the Bible, the individuals who decided what should be in the Bible based their decisions on what they thought was the right way to believe! There were divergent views early on, and it was the views of the proto-orthodox which won out.

To put it as succinctly as I can:

- Many people today believe the only way to get correct knowledge about God and Jesus is through the Bible, but the content of the Bible was determined by people who made the decision about what was the right way to believe.

Or

- Many people believe it's "correct belief" because it's in the Bible, when in fact it's in the Bible because it was considered "correct belief" by a group of individuals who had the power to make such decisions.

There still are controversies about what belongs in the canon. The canons of the Roman Catholics, the Protestants, and the Orthodox are all different. Muslims added a third testament, the Qur'an. Mormons added a third testament, the

Book of Mormon. Thomas Jefferson disagreed with what was put in the Bible and took out all of the Scripture he felt did not belong. Others recently have advocated opening the canon up for new additions based on new archaeological discoveries of Scripture that were not available during the time the New Testament canon was formulated in the second through fourth centuries.

Many evangelicals and fundamentalists believe that the words of the Bible are the literal words of God and without error. If that is true, it involves a tremendous amount of people who are not making errors. This would include:

- The many individuals who wrote the books that made it into our canon.
- The many individuals who decided what should be in our canon and what should be excluded.
- The thousands of people who made hand written copies of the Bible before the invention of the printing press.
- The thousands of people who were involved in translating the Bible from the original Hebrew and Greek into the over 2,000 languages it has been translated into.

As a result of extensive study and research, I do not interpret the Bible as the literal words of God, but I do take it seriously. I do not worship and venerate the Bible. I worship and venerate God. I think Scripture has great value, and this includes writings that did not make it into the canon as well as those that did. I object strongly to the concept of *sola scriptura*, i.e., that the Bible is the only way to know about God. I believe strongly in the tools of science in learning about God and God's creation. I believe in slogans of the

Christian denomination in which I belong, the United Church of Christ, which says "God is still speaking." I believe revelations did not end in the first century C.E. but continue to this day. Another slogan of the UCC is "Never put a period where God has placed a coma." I continue to seek God's ongoing revelations.

Look for the second book in this series, entitled "Evolution of Religion" which explores the development of religion from prehistoric times. The book particularly will investigate the influences of various cultures on the development of both Judaism and Christianity.

Group Discussion Questions

Group Discussion Questions
Worldview

Group Session #1: Preface, Introduction, and Chapter 1

- What was your early worldview like? How was your own early worldview similar or different from the author's in the Preface of this book?

- Is your current worldview different from your early worldview? In what ways?

- What are your beliefs about the Bible?

- What are your favorite books in the Bible? Least favorite? Why?

- Does the Bible have relevance for us in the 21st century? All of it?

- What does it mean to be "inspired" by God? Is there anything else that is "inspired" by God?

Group Discussion Questions
Judaism and the Intertestamental Period

Group Session #2: Chapters 2 and 3

- Do you see a change or evolution in Judaism as time goes by, or do you see Judaism as being exactly the same religion throughout its history? Was Judaism the same in its beginnings as it is now? Explain.

- Was there any evolution in the Jews' conception of God?

- Do you agree with the author's assertion that the ten commandments were addressed specifically to the Jewish population, and not the world at large? Do you think that these are the most important rules we should follow to serve God? If you were going to write the ten most important commandments what would they be?

- What was the purpose of sacrifice in Judaism? Is there still a role for sacrifice?

- Do you believe it is necessary to make a "payment" for sins and mistakes? Does forgiveness require a price? Apply this to our legal system.

- Do you believe the Jews were/are God's chosen people?

Group Discussion Questions
Christianity

Group Session #3: Chapter 4

- Were you surprised to learn that Christianity was so varied in its early years?

- What does it mean to you to be a Christian?

- How important are various miracles to your faith, such as the virgin birth, miraculous healings, raising Lazarus from the dead?

- What is the significance of Jesus dying on the cross for you?

- How important is a physical resurrection of Jesus after his death for your faith?

- What is "salvation" to you? What is your conception of heaven? Who gets saved? Do you believe in "election" and predestination? Do you believe in universal salvation?

- Do the various gospels present differing conceptions of Jesus? How are they the same and different?

- Who is Jesus Christ?

Group Discussion Questions
Forming the Bible

Group Session #4: Chapter 5

- Overall, any thoughts or feelings about the information presented in this book?

- Has the information in this book affected your worldview? Has it affected your faith in any way?

- Are there any books of the Bible that you don't think belong, or any writings that you think should have been included?

- What effect do politics have on biblical interpretations?

- What are your thoughts about the author's conclusions in the Postface?

- What are your thoughts about the Bible's ability to answer questions not just about God but about other areas of inquiry, for example geology, biology, astronomy, etc.?

- What are your thoughts about "special revelation" (belief that the knowledge of God can be achieved through supernatural means, i.e., God speaking directly to certain special individuals)?

Bibliography and Recommendations
for Further Reading

Borg, Marcus J., and Crossan, John D. (2007). *The First Christmas: What the Gospels Really Teach About Jesus's Birth.* New York: HarperCollins.

Borg, Marcus J., and Crossan, John D. (2009). *The First Paul: Reclaiming the Radical Visionary Behind the Church's Conservative Icon.* New York: HarperCollins.

Borg, Marcus J. (2012). *Evolution of the Word.* New York: HarperCollins.

Coogan, Michael D. (2011). *The Old Testament: A Historical and Literary Introduction to the Hebrew Scriptures,* 2nd edition. New York: Oxford University Press.

Ehrman, Bart D. (2003). *Lost Christianities: The Battles for Scripture and the Faiths We Never Knew.* New York: Oxford University Press.

Ehrman, Bart D. (2011). *The Orthodox Corruption of Scripture.* New York: Oxford University Press.

Ehrman, Bart D. (2012). *The New Testament: A Historical Introduction to the Early Christian Writings,* 5th edition. New York: Oxford University Press.

Ehrman, Bart D. (2015). *After the New Testament: A Reader in Early Christianity 100-300 C.E.,* 2nd edition. New York: Oxford University Press.

Metzger, Bruce M. (1987). *The Canon of the New Testament: Its Origin, Development and Significance.* New York: Oxford University Press.

Metzger, Bruce M. (2001). *The Bible in Translation: Ancient and English Versions.* Grand Rapids: Baker Academic.
The Anchor Bible Dictionary (1992).

The Harper Collins Study Bible (2006). New York: HarperCollins.

Index

54588147R00105

Made in the USA
Charleston, SC
08 April 2016